M000302839

The McNutt Family

THIS BOOK BELONGS TO

Mom

PRESENTED BY

Nov. 2013

DATE

Fondue!

Rice Krispies
lemon cupcakes
brownies
pizza sized cookie -Pin.
lemon butter cookies
ginger cookies - Pin.
Paula Deen choc. chip Ooey gooey cake
cookie brownies

Illustrated
BIBLE STORIES
for Latter-day Saints

Illustrated
BIBLE STORIES
for Latter-day Saints

Retold by Karmel H. Newell
Illustrated by Brian Call

DESERET
BOOK

Salt Lake City, Utah

About the Author

Karmel Newell holds bachelor's and master's degrees in English literature. She has served on a general Church writing committee, as a Relief Society president, and as a Primary president. She has written other books for children and loves being with children—her own and others. Whether reading Bible stories or hiking mountain trails, Karmel loves spending time with her husband, Lloyd, and their family.

About the Illustrator

Brian Call graduated from Brigham Young University with a bachelor's degree in fine arts. Since that time, he has worked as an illustrator, creating artwork that has appeared in numerous magazines, books, and educational materials. He currently teaches in the art department at Brigham Young University–Idaho in Rexburg, Idaho. Brian and his wife, Michelle, and their six children live in Ammon, Idaho.

Text © 2013 Karmel H. Newell
Illustrations © 2013 Brian Call

Visit us at DeseretBook.com

Library of Congress Cataloging-in-Publication Data
Newell, Karmel H., author.
   Illustrated Bible stories for Latter-day Saints / retold by Karmel H. Newell ; Illustrated by Brian Call.
      pages cm
   Includes bibliographical references and index.
   ISBN 978-1-60907-717-4 (hardbound : alk. paper) 1. Bible stories, English. I. Call, Brian D., illustrator. II. Title.
   BS550.3.N49 2013
   220.95'05—dc23   2013023293

Printed in China   09/13
R. R. Donnelley, Shenzhen, Guangdong, China

10   9   8   7   6   5   4   3   2   1

To my children and my children's children
—Karmel H. Newell

To my wonderful wife, Michelle, and my children
—Brian Call

Contents

How to Use This Book

This book is intended to supplement, not replace, scripture study. The spiritual power that comes from reading the word of God directly from the scriptures cannot come from any other source. However, spiritual insight and power can flow more freely when readers know more about people, places, and events described in the scriptures. As readers—especially young readers—become familiar with scripture stories, the doctrines and truths illustrated by those stories are more easily understood.

The stories in this book are arranged in historical order. Each chapter contains a separate story with sidebars that explain important concepts, introduce essential vocabulary, or offer background facts. The sidebars may be read before, during, or after the story.

Uses for this book are as varied as the families who read it. If, for example, a family conducts scripture study in the morning, this book might be used for bedtime stories to reinforce what was learned earlier in the day. If a family gathers for scripture study at night, this book may be placed in a central location in the home, so children can refer to it to supplement their knowledge on their own. *Illustrated Bible Stories for Latter-day Saints* certainly provides the framework for a series of family home evenings. Because Bible events are retold as stories, this book may also lend itself well to discussion and to bearing testimony of gospel principles illuminated therein.

Family Home Evening Suggestions

At least a year's worth of family home evening lessons may be found in this book. Each chapter is a self-contained lesson. The sidebars offer important supplementary information, the illustrations engage younger children in the stories, and the stories themselves can be read aloud or retold.

Families with younger children may enjoy reading a story together and then acting out what they read. Children might prepare simple costumes and take turns playing the various characters. "Tents" might be made of sheets, strips of fabric might become the sea or the wilderness, stairs might depict Jacob's ladder, and so forth. The scriptures will come to life as children become familiar with a story by acting it out.

Families with older children might enjoy connecting scripture stories with the teachings of modern prophets. A search on lds.org can link a scripture story with a talk given by a prophet or with an article published in a Church magazine. As older children prepare to teach a family home evening lesson, they might first read the retelling of the scripture story in the book and then tie it to a gospel truth.

Parents may use this book in teaching gospel topics. The format of this book allows for a quick review of the stories, and the stories may serve as springboards for family discussion. The Lord's admonition to the Israelites resounds through the ages: "Thou shalt love the Lord with all thine heart, . . . and these words, which I command thee this day, shall be in thine heart: And thou shalt teach them diligently unto thy children, and shalt talk of them when thou sittest in thine house, and when thou walkest by the way, and when thou liest down, and when thou risest up" (Deuteronomy 6:5–7).

The Creation

God, our Heavenly Father, chose His spirit Son, Jesus Christ, to help Him create heaven and the earth. At first, the earth was empty and barren. Darkness spread across the deep, and God's spirit moved upon the water. God said, "Let there be light, and there was light." God saw the light, and He knew it was good. He divided the light from the darkness. That was the first day of creation.

On the second day of creation, God divided the waters, so there was water in the firmament, or sky, and also in the great waters beneath the firmament, or on the earth. God called the firmament "Heaven."

On the third day of creation, God gathered the great waters on the earth into one place and said, "Let there be dry land." God called the dry land "Earth," and He called the gathering together of the waters "Seas."

God also made the grass, trees, and other plants; they brought forth fruit and seeds. God saw all the things He had made, and He declared that they were good.

On the fourth day of creation, God placed lights in the sky. He made two great lights: the sun to rule the day and the moon to rule the night. He also put stars in the sky. The lights divided the day from the night, and they became signs in the heavens of the seasons, years, and days.

On the fifth day of creation, God placed fish in the sea and birds in the sky. He blessed the fish and birds and said to them, "Be fruitful, and multiply."

On the sixth day, God created all the animals and creeping things. Then God, our Heavenly Father, said to Jesus Christ, "Let us make man in our image." So God created Adam, the first man on the earth. Heavenly Father and Jesus knew that it was not good for man to be alone, so they created a woman, who was named Eve, to help Adam and to be his wife. God made Adam and Eve caretakers of the fish, birds, animals, and creeping things. God blessed Adam and Eve and told them to have children. God saw everything he had made and declared that it was very good.

On the seventh day, God rested from all his work. He blessed the seventh day and made it sacred.

Days of Creation

A day was not twenty-four hours long, as we measure it. We do not know exactly how long a day of creation was, but it was probably much longer than one of our days. The Apostle Peter taught, for example, that "one day is with the Lord as a thousand years, and a thousand years as one day" (2 Peter 3:8).

Adam and Eve

Garden of Eden

This beautiful place was a paradise, where people and animals lived together in peace (McConkie, "Christ and the Creation," 9–15).

God planted lovely, fruitful trees and other plants in a place called Eden. He caused lovely and fruitful trees and other plants to grow there. God brought the animals and birds to Adam, and Adam gave each one a name. Adam and Eve lived in the Garden of Eden and took care of all of the plants and animals.

Two of the trees in the garden, the tree of life and the tree of knowledge of good and evil, were very unusual. God had told Adam and Eve that they could eat from any of the trees in the garden—except the tree of knowledge of good and evil. He told them that if they chose to eat from that tree, they would die.

Like a snake, Satan, or the devil, came to Eve and lied to her. Satan told her that she and Adam would not die if they ate fruit from the tree of knowledge of good and evil. But he mixed that lie with some truth: he told her that if she ate the fruit, she would know the difference between good and evil. Eve decided to eat the forbidden fruit, and then she gave some to Adam.

After they ate fruit from the tree of knowledge of good and evil, Adam and Eve were able to understand and recognize things they had not known before. One thing they now realized was that they were naked. When the Lord called out to them, Adam and Eve hid from Him. The Lord asked them if they had eaten the fruit he had told them not to eat. Adam and Eve admitted that they had.

Because they had eaten the forbidden fruit, Adam and Eve were no longer pure and clean before God, and they would someday die. God said that Adam and Eve would have to leave the Garden of Eden. He placed cherubim and a flaming sword to guard the tree of life so that Adam and Eve could no longer eat its fruit. If they ate fruit from the tree of life after eating from the tree of knowledge of good and evil, they would be unclean forever. God wanted them to have the opportunity to repent. He made coats of animal skins for them to wear and led them out of the Garden of Eden. Life in the mortal world would not be easy, and they would have to work hard—but now they would be able to have children.

Cherubim

Cherubim are beings who guard sacred things (OT student manual 1:148).

Adam and Eve's Family

Altar

Usually built of stones, an altar was a structure where people knelt and offered prayers to God or where they offered animal sacrifices.

When Adam and Eve left the Garden of Eden, Adam began plowing the ground so that he could plant seeds and grow food. Adam and Eve had sons and daughters, and they worked together to raise their family and take care of the animals.

Adam and Eve lived righteously and prayed to Heavenly Father. God commanded them to worship Him and to build an altar and offer sacrifices. Adam obeyed and began giving the best of his flocks as an offering to the Lord. After many days, an angel came to Adam and asked him why he was offering sacrifices to the Lord. Adam said, "I know not, save the Lord commanded me." Even though he didn't know why the Lord had asked him to do this, Adam wanted to be obedient. The angel explained that Adam's sacrifices would remind his family of the great sacrifice that Jesus Christ would someday make in giving his life for all people. The angel taught Adam to repent and to do everything in the name of the Son of God.

Sacrifices

To sacrifice means to offer or give up something valuable as a way of showing our love for God and our willingness to do what is right. According to the commandment, Adam and Eve gave some of the best of what they had to God. These sacrifices helped them to understand the great sacrifice that would be made by the Son of God. In our day, we take the sacrament to remind us that Jesus Christ gave the ultimate sacrifice of His perfect life.

Some of Adam and Eve's children chose to obey their parents and follow the Lord, and some chose to follow Satan. One of their sons, Cain, became a farmer who worked in the fields. He loved Satan more than he loved God. Another son, Abel, was a shepherd who took care of the animals. He obeyed the Lord's commandments. When it came time for them to offer sacrifices to the Lord, Abel obeyed the law and gave his very best sheep. But Cain listened to Satan and did not offer a proper sacrifice. The Lord was not pleased with Cain's offering.

Cain became angry and stopped listening to the Lord or to his parents or the other righteous members of his family. Cain listened to Satan and secretly talked with him. Cain decided to kill Abel.

After Abel was dead, Cain was proud of the evil he had done and thought that now his brother's flocks would be his. When the Lord asked Cain where his brother Abel was, Cain rudely answered, "Am I my brother's keeper?" The Lord knew that Cain had killed Abel, and He cursed Cain. He told Cain that the ground would no longer grow food for him and that he would have to wander the earth for the rest of his life. Cain and his family moved far away. Adam and Eve's family was no longer together.

The Prophet Enoch

Methuselah

Methuselah was Enoch's son who remained on the earth when the city of Enoch was taken to heaven. He was a righteous man and continued to teach the people. He lived to be 969 years old and was the great-grandfather of Noah.

Enoch came from a righteous family. His father and grandfather and several grandfathers before them were all good men. They taught the people to repent and to have faith in Jesus Christ.

One day, while Enoch was traveling away from the land of Cainan, he had a vision, and he heard the voice of the Lord. The Lord wanted Enoch to tell the people to repent. Enoch bowed down and asked the Lord why he had been chosen to be God's messenger. Enoch was only a young man, and he did not think he was a good speaker. The Lord promised Enoch that if he would obey and open his mouth, the Lord would help him speak.

The Lord told Enoch to place clay on his eyelids and then wash them, and by the power of God he would be able to see more than he could before. After Enoch washed the clay off his eyes, he became known as a seer because he could see the spirits that God had created, things that had happened in the past, things that would happen in the future, and other things that were not visible to the natural eye.

Zion

Zion means "the pure in heart." It may refer to a place where people who are pure in heart live, or it may describe the people who live there. The tenth article of faith tells us that a new city called "Zion (the New Jerusalem) will be built upon the American continent" before Jesus comes again.

Below: Mount Zion in Jerusalem

Enoch went among the people and testified against their evil works. Many of the people did not like what he said, but no one dared lay hands on him. They knew he was a man of God. Enoch reminded them of the book of remembrance, or history, that had been kept of God's dealings with the people on earth. He taught them about faith in Jesus Christ, repentance, and baptism. As Enoch spoke the words of God, the people trembled and could not stand in his presence.

Enoch climbed Mount Simeon, and the heavens opened to his view. He saw the Lord and talked with him face to face. The Lord commanded Enoch to preach repentance. Those who believed in Enoch's words were baptized and became known as the people of God. Enoch's faith was so great that he led the people of God in battle as they defended themselves against their enemies. When he spoke, mountains moved, rivers changed their course, and land rose out of the depths of the sea. The wicked people were afraid and stayed away from Enoch and the people of God.

Enoch and his people were blessed by the Lord. They lived together in righteousness in a city called Zion. They shared what they had with each other, and no one among them was poor. They became so pure and holy that the Lord took Enoch and his people up to heaven.

Noah and the Ark

Noah and his family lived on the earth nearly seven hundred years after the city of Enoch was taken to heaven. Noah had three sons: Japheth, Shem, and Ham, who married and had many children of their own. Noah's sons kept the commandments and lived together in righteousness, but most of the other people on the earth did not.

The Lord told Noah to warn the people that His Spirit would not remain with them if they did not repent of their sins. For 120 years, Noah warned them to turn from their violence and wickedness, or they would be destroyed. No one but Noah's family would listen to him.

Finally, at the end of that time, the Lord told Noah to build an ark of gopher wood. He instructed Noah how big to make the ark, where to put a window and a door, and to build it three stories high. The Lord told Noah that there would be a great flood and that everything on the earth would die. He commanded Noah to take into the ark male and female of every living creature: birds, beasts, and creeping things. He also told Noah to pack food for his family and for all of the animals.

Then it started to rain. It rained for forty days and forty nights. Noah and his family and the animals and birds were safe inside the ark, but everything else was destroyed. The flood waters lifted the ark off the ground, causing it to float in the deep water. All the high hills and even the mountains were covered. The waters covered the earth for 150 days.

At last, the fountains of the deep and the windows of heaven dried up, and the waters stopped. Months after the flood began, the ark rested on the mountains of Ararat. The waters decreased for several more months until the tops of the mountains became visible.

After forty more days had passed, Noah opened the window of the ark and sent out a dove. It found no place to rest, and it came back to the ark. A week later, Noah sent the dove out again. Later that day, the dove returned with an olive leaf in its mouth, and Noah knew the water level was going down. Another week later, Noah sent the dove out again, and this time the dove did not return. It had found a new home. Noah opened the door and saw that the ground was dry. He and his family and all of the animals left the ark where they had lived for more than a year.

Noah built an altar and offered prayers of thanks to God. The Lord made a covenant with Noah, promising that He would never again cover the whole earth with water. He told Noah that the rainbow in the sky would be a token, or sign, of this covenant.

Dimensions of the Ark

The ark was about 450 feet long, 75 feet wide, and 45 feet high. It was probably about one and a half football fields long (OT student manual 1:54–55).

Long Lives

Noah was six hundred years old when the flood started. We do not know why people lived so many years in ancient times. It appears that after the flood people lived shorter lives (Holzapfel et al., *World,* 25).

The Tower of Babel

Ziggurat

The tower of Babel may have looked like a ziggurat, a pyramid-like structure that became common in Middle Eastern countries thousands of years ago. Ziggurats were built with thousands of bricks that were made of mud and straw, poured into wooden casts, and then baked in the sun or in an oven. Ziggurats usually had a temple at the top and another at the base (Holzapfel et al., *World,* 30).

Noah and his family left the ark in the mountains and moved to a flat land called Shinar. Hundreds of years passed, and Noah's three sons and their families had children, grandchildren, and great-grandchildren. They became a great people. Everyone on the earth spoke the same language.

The people learned how to shape and bake clay into hard bricks to make houses and other buildings. They built a city called Babel. In Babel, the people decided to raise a huge tower of bricks so high that it would reach heaven. They did not understand that the only way to get to heaven is to obey God.

When the Lord saw the city and the tower they built, he was not pleased. They had forgotten the Lord and relied too much on their own strength. The Lord decided to confuse their language so they could not understand each other when they spoke.

When the people began speaking different languages, they divided up, left Shinar, and scattered abroad across the earth.

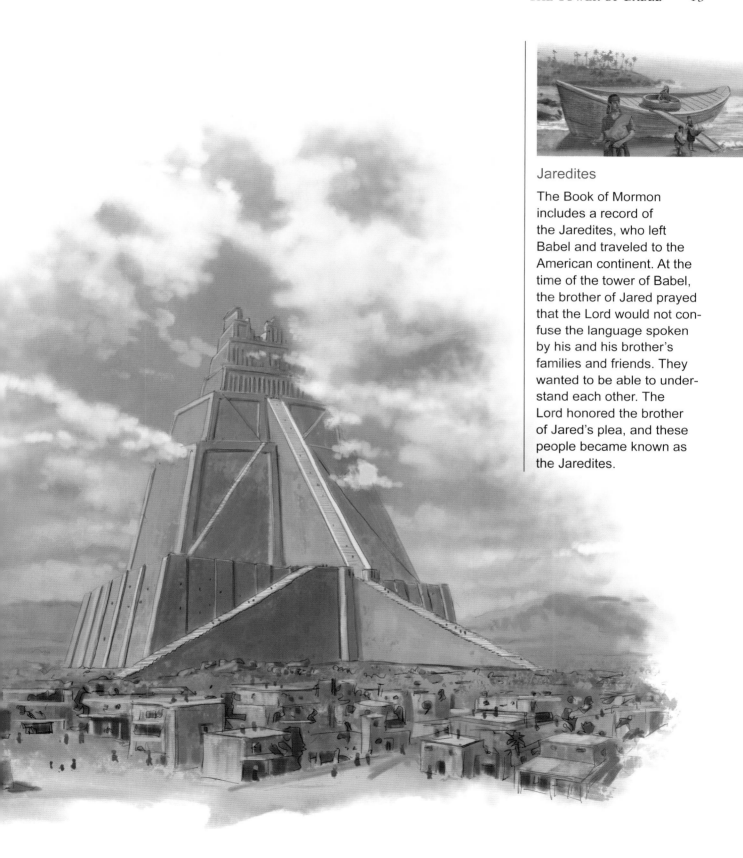

Jaredites

The Book of Mormon includes a record of the Jaredites, who left Babel and traveled to the American continent. At the time of the tower of Babel, the brother of Jared prayed that the Lord would not confuse the language spoken by his and his brother's families and friends. They wanted to be able to understand each other. The Lord honored the brother of Jared's plea, and these people became known as the Jaredites.

The Prophet Abraham

Melchizedek

A high priest who lived more than 4,000 years ago, Melchizedek was the king of Salem (later known as Jerusalem). Even though he lived among wicked people, he led them to repent, and as a result they had peace in the land. The Book of Mormon prophet Alma wrote that no one was greater than Melchizedek (Alma 13:19). The proper name of the higher priesthood is *the Holy Priesthood, after the Order of the Son of God.* But the people wanted to show reverence for God by not repeating his name too often, so they began calling this priesthood the Melchizedek Priesthood to honor Melchizedek and his righteousness (D&C 107:2–4).

Abraham and his family lived in the land of Ur. Some of Abraham's family were righteous, and some were not. Abraham wanted to do what was right, and he wanted to receive the priesthood. But Abraham's father, Terah, was not righteous. Terah worshipped idols. When the wicked priests tried to sacrifice Abraham on an altar, Terah did not try to stop them. Abraham prayed for help, and the Lord came to his rescue. An angel freed Abraham and helped him escape. The Lord spoke to Abraham and told him to leave the land of his fathers.

Abraham and his wife, Sarah, along with Abraham's nephew Lot and his wife and their families, left Ur and settled in the land of Haran. Because Ur was struck by a great famine (a time when there is no food), Abraham's father, Terah, followed Abraham to Haran. After a time, the Lord instructed Abraham to continue his journey and go to the land of Canaan. Lot and his family went with Abraham, but Terah stayed in Haran and turned once again to idolatry.

Abraham prayed for the people who stayed behind. The Lord continued to bless Abraham, leading him and Lot to the land of Egypt when the famine spread to Canaan. In Egypt, there was plenty of food and water, and Abraham prospered.

Years later, when Abraham and Lot left Egypt and returned to the land of Canaan, they had become rich in cattle, silver, and gold. They decided to divide the land between them. Lot took his family to a well-watered plain called Jordan, and Abraham settled with his family in Hebron.

One day, Abraham learned that several kings in the land where Lot lived were at war with one another. During one of the battles, Lot and his people were captured. Abraham took 318 of his men and went to Lot's rescue, freeing Lot and his people and returning them to their homes.

On his way back to his own land, Abraham met Melchizedek, the king of Salem. Melchizedek was a very righteous man. Because he held the priesthood, he blessed Abraham and ordained him to the priesthood. At last, Abraham held the authority of God, as he had long desired. The Lord made great promises to Abraham. Not only did He give Abraham the land of Canaan but He also promised him that the whole earth would be blessed through Abraham's descendants and that someday Jesus Christ would be born through Abraham's family.

Idolatry

When people worship something else instead of God, such as nature (the sun, moon, stars, rivers, or animals) or man-made images (statues or pictures), their worship is called idolatry.

Abraham and Isaac

Living in a Tent

Like Abraham and his family, many desert dwellers lived in tents because they constantly moved to new fields where their flocks could find food. The tents may have been made of coarse goat hair to make the tents waterproof (Olson, *Women,* 26).

When Abraham was ninety-nine years old, the Lord appeared to him and made a covenant, or special promise, that Abraham would be the father of many nations and that the whole earth would be blessed through his family. Before the covenant, Abraham's name was Abram, and Sarah's name was Sarai. The Lord changed their names to remind them of the covenant He had made with them. The name *Abraham* means "father of many"; *Sarah* means "princess."

When he heard the Lord promise that he would be a father, Abraham fell to the ground and laughed with joy. But he wondered how this could possibly happen— Sarah, his wife, was ninety years old! The Lord assured Abraham that Sarah would bear a son and told him that they should name him Isaac. Abraham promised to obey.

In the heat of the day, Abraham was sitting in the doorway to his tent, with his head down. When he looked up, he saw three holy men. Abraham ran to meet them and bowed down before them. He brought water to wash the desert dust from their feet and asked Sarah to prepare food for them.

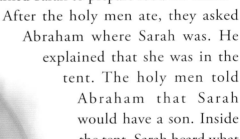

After the holy men ate, they asked Abraham where Sarah was. He explained that she was in the tent. The holy men told Abraham that Sarah would have a son. Inside the tent, Sarah heard what they said and laughed to herself, wondering how a woman as old as she was could have a baby. But the Lord again assured Abraham, "Is anything too hard for the Lord?"

In time, Sarah did give birth to a son, and she and Abraham named him Isaac. They watched him grow, and they held a feast for him. They loved him very much.

When Isaac was a young man, the Lord desired to test Abraham. He told Abraham to take his son Isaac to Mount Moriah and offer him there as a sacrifice. Abraham rose early the next morning, packed his donkey, and took Isaac, along with two other young men, on the three-day journey to the mountain. Abraham told the young men to wait at the foot of the mount, and he climbed up with Isaac. Abraham and Isaac carried wood, a torch for fire, and a knife. When Isaac asked his father where the lamb for the burnt offering was, Abraham simply answered that God would provide a lamb.

Abraham tied Isaac with rope and laid him on the wood on the altar. Just as Abraham stretched out his hand and lifted the knife, an angel called out to him and told him to stop. The angel said that Abraham had proven he was willing to give anything, even his promised son, to the Lord. Then Abraham noticed a ram whose horns were caught in a nearby bush. Abraham offered the ram on the altar and thanked the Lord for sparing his precious son.

Mount Moriah

Mount Moriah is a prominent hill in Jerusalem. It is in the same area where, almost two thousand years later, Jesus Christ offered his perfect life as a sacrifice for us (OT student manual 1:77).

Lot and His Wife

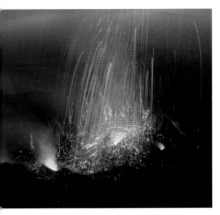

Fire and Brimstone

The Lord sent down fire and burning substances, such as sulfur, like rain upon Sodom and Gomorrah. Because the wicked people were destroyed by these elements, "fire and brimstone" have become symbols of God's anger.

When Abraham left his home in Ur, his nephew Lot traveled with him. Lot stayed with Abraham for several years. Like his uncle, Lot was a good man. Eventually, Abraham and Lot had to separate because they both needed more land for their cattle. Lot and his wife and family settled a flat area by the Jordan River, near the cities of Sodom and Gomorrah. Even though Lot and his family were righteous, the people in Sodom and Gomorrah had become very wicked.

The Lord came to Abraham and told him that Sodom and Gomorrah were going to be destroyed. Abraham asked the Lord if he would spare Sodom as long as fifty righteous people lived there. The Lord said that he would. Abraham asked the Lord if he would spare the city if only forty-five, forty, thirty, twenty, or even just ten righteous people could be found. The Lord said that he would not destroy the city if as few as ten righteous people remained—but there were not even ten righteous people to be found in Sodom!

The Lord sent three angels, or holy men, to warn Lot, his wife, and his family that the cities of Sodom and Gomorrah were going to be destroyed. Lot went to meet the angels. He bowed down before them, invited them into his home, and persuaded them not to spend the night in the street. As soon as the angels went inside, wicked men surrounded Lot's home and yelled for him to send the holy men out. Lot went out to talk with the angry people, but they pressed upon Lot and almost broke his door. The holy men reached outside the door and pulled Lot back inside. They struck the men outside with blindness. When they could no longer find the door, the intruders went away.

Once the wicked men had left, Lot tried to warn his married daughters and their husbands that Sodom and Gomorrah were going to be destroyed. Sadly, they did not believe his warnings.

Early the next morning, the angels told Lot and his wife and his two other daughters to hurry away to safety. When they were taking too long, the angels finally took them by their hands and brought them out of the city. They told Lot and his family to run for their lives and warned them not to look back.

The Lord rained fire and brimstone on Sodom and Gomorrah. The cities went up in smoke and were completely destroyed. Even though Lot's wife had been warned, she did look back—and she was turned into a pillar of salt. Lot and his two daughters left the city and found safety in a nearby mountain cave.

A Pillar of Salt

While it is not clear what is meant by Lot's wife becoming a "pillar of salt," we know that she died after she looked, or maybe even turned back, to Sodom. The place where these cities were located is now part of the Dead Sea, a lake that is too salty for anything to live in it. Perhaps Lot's wife becoming "a pillar of salt" means that she died there and was eventually swallowed by the Dead Sea (OT student manual 1:67, 76–77).

Isaac and Rebekah

Arranged Marriages

Anciently, young adults did not usually choose whom they would marry. Their parents arranged for them to marry someone in the community, often in their own extended family.

When Abraham was an old man, he asked his eldest servant to find a wife for his son Isaac. Abraham did not want Isaac to marry a Canaanite. He hoped to find a wife for Isaac who worshipped God as his family did. He asked his servant to look for a wife for Isaac in Haran, where Abraham's extended family lived, about 850 miles, or a month's journey, away.

Abraham's servant asked Abraham what he should do if the woman did not want to return to Canaan with him. Abraham assured the servant that the Lord would send an angel to prepare the way for him. The servant made an oath, or promise, that he would do as Abraham asked. The servant took ten of his master's camels and traveled to Haran.

When he arrived in Haran, the camels needed water, and the servant led them to the village well. It was evening, the time of day when the women of the town came to draw water for their households. The servant prayed that the Lord would be merciful to his master and bless Isaac

with a good wife. He prayed that the Lord would let him know who the young woman would be. The servant told the Lord that he was going to ask a young woman to give him water to drink. If she agreed to give him water—and then offered to bring water for his camels, too—the servant would know that she should be the chosen bride for Isaac. The servant prayed that the Lord would let this be a sign that he had found the right woman.

A very beautiful young woman named Rebekah came to the well and filled her pitcher. The servant approached her and asked her for some water. She quickly responded by giving him a drink from her pitcher. When he had finished drinking, Rebekah immediately offered to draw water for all of his camels. She filled her pitcher many times to provide enough water for all of the camels.

When the camels were satisfied, the servant gave Rebekah a golden earring and two bracelets, and he asked who her parents were. When she told him that her grandfather was Nahor, who was Abraham's brother, the servant knew his prayer had been answered. He had found a wife for Isaac from Abraham's own family.

The servant went with Rebekah to her home and talked with her family. He asked that Rebekah be Isaac's wife. After her family heard about how the Lord had answered the servant's prayer, they knew that he had been guided to Rebekah. They agreed to the marriage, and Rebekah agreed to leave her home to become Isaac's wife.

Well of Water

In the ancient world, a community shared a well of water. At least twice a day, women carried pitchers to the well to obtain water for cooking and washing and for watering their animals (Olson, *Women,* 51–53).

Jacob and Esau

Birthright

Anciently, the firstborn son received the birthright, or the right to inherit land and authority to be the leader of the family.

Jacob

The name *Jacob* means "supplanter," or one who takes the place of another.

Isaac was forty years old when he married Rebekah. Isaac prayed that his wife would be able to have children, but it was twenty years before Rebekah became pregnant—with twins. She felt the two babies struggling inside her, and she prayed to understand why. The Lord told her that two nations would come from these twins. One of the nations would be stronger than the other, and the older one would serve the younger.

Rebekah gave birth to Esau first. His coloring was red, and he was covered with hair. After the second baby was born, he took hold of Esau's heel. They named the second boy Jacob. Esau grew to be a skilled hunter and man of the field. Jacob grew to be a good man, and he lived in a tent.

One day Esau came in from the field, faint with hunger. Jacob had just made some pottage, or stew. Esau asked Jacob to give him some of the stew. Jacob said that he would—if Esau gave Jacob his birthright, or his inheritance. Esau did not care about his birthright, so he traded it for a bowl of stew. Esau showed that he also didn't care about God's promises when he married a woman who did not worship the true God the way his family did. Isaac and Rebekah were sad about Esau's decision. They hoped their second son, Jacob, would marry someone who made and kept promises with God.

Isaac became old and could not see well. He asked Esau to go hunting and bring him some meat to give him strength to give Esau a blessing before he died. Rebekah overheard Isaac talking with Esau. She knew that Jacob, not Esau, should receive the blessing, so she quickly thought of a plan. While Esau was hunting, Rebekah told Jacob to bring her two goats from their flock so she could cook them, and Jacob, instead of Esau, could give tasty meat to his father. She also put skin from the goats on Jacob's hands and neck. Then, when his father touched him, Jacob would feel hairy like his brother, Esau.

Jacob brought the meat to his father. Isaac asked him to come close to him. Isaac felt Jacob's hands and neck. They were hairy like Esau's, but Isaac thought the voice he heard sounded like Jacob's. Isaac kissed Jacob, and he smelled like the field, as Esau did. When Isaac finished eating, he gave Jacob a great blessing, telling him that he would rule over many people and nations.

When Esau came back from hunting, he discovered that his father had given Jacob the blessing he thought he deserved. Esau was very angry with Jacob and even threatened to kill him. Rebekah told Jacob to leave their home and find safety in Haran with her brother, Laban, until Esau's anger had cooled.

Twenty years later, Jacob was returning to his home country. He sent messengers to tell Esau that he was coming and to offer him gifts. The messengers returned with the news that Esau was on his way to meet Jacob—and that there were 400 men with him. Jacob was worried that Esau was still angry, and when he came near, Jacob bowed down seven times as a way of showing his love and respect. But Esau ran to meet Jacob. He hugged him and kissed him, and the two brothers wept and expressed their love for each other.

Jacob and Rachel

Jacob's Ladder

One night during his journey to Haran to find a wife, Jacob dreamed about a ladder that reached to heaven. The rungs on the ladder represented the covenants that lead us to God (OT student manual 1:86). Like Jacob, we are blessed by keeping our covenants.

Before Jacob left for Haran, Isaac talked with him. He asked Jacob to promise not to marry a Canaanite, because the Canaanite people worshipped idols and did not believe in the true God. Like Jacob's mother, Rebekah, Isaac wanted Jacob to go to Haran, the land where Jacob's uncle Laban lived, and find a wife among those who believed in God.

As Jacob journeyed toward Haran, he came upon a well of water in a field. He asked the men who had come to water their sheep if they knew Laban. Not only did they know him but they also pointed out Laban's daughter Rachel, who at that very moment was walking toward the well with her father's sheep. When Jacob saw Rachel coming, he rolled the large stone away from the well and watered the sheep for her.

Jacob greeted Rachel with a kiss. As he talked with her, he wept tears of joy, and he explained how their families were related. She ran to tell her father, Laban. When Laban heard that Jacob had come, he ran to meet him. Laban embraced Jacob and took him to his house.

After Jacob had stayed with Laban and worked for their family for a month, Laban asked Jacob how he could pay him for his work. Jacob said that he would work for free if only he could marry Laban's beautiful daughter Rachel. Laban agreed to give his daughter to Jacob if he worked for him for seven years.

Seven years later, Laban hosted a wedding feast for Jacob. After the feast, Laban brought his older daughter, Leah, instead of Rachel, to marry Jacob. He told Jacob that their custom did not allow the younger daughter to marry before the older daughter. Laban told Jacob that he could marry Rachel, too, if he would stay and work for seven more years. Jacob loved Rachel so much that he agreed.

After they were married, Rachel was unable to have children for a long time. Isaac and Rachel prayed, and the Lord answered their prayers. At last, Rachel gave birth to a son they named Joseph. Several years later, when the family no longer lived in Haran, Rachel died while giving birth to another son, named Benjamin.

Tithing

When Jacob awoke from his dream about the ladder that reached to heaven, he built an altar of stone and made a promise that he would give one-tenth of everything he had to the Lord.

The Twelve Sons of Jacob

Israel

The name *Israel* is used to mean three things: (1) the name of the man Jacob, (2) another name for the land of Canaan, and (3) a people who are true believers in Jesus Christ and who make and keep covenants with Him (Bible Dictionary, 708).

The Coat of Many Colors

Probably very costly to make, this may have been a long coat with long sleeves. It may have shown that Joseph, instead of the oldest son, received the birthright blessing (OT student manual 1:89, 93).

After many years of living among Laban's family, Jacob was commanded by the Lord to return to Canaan, the land that had been promised to Jacob's father and grandfather. By this time, Jacob had a large family and many animals and servants. One night during the journey, Jacob was visited by a heavenly messenger. The messenger blessed Jacob and told him that his name would be changed from *Jacob* to *Israel*.

Jacob and his family settled in Canaan, and Jacob's brother, Esau, lived in a nearby land. There was peace between them, and later, when their father, Isaac, died, they came together to bury him.

Once again, the Lord visited Jacob and blessed him. The Lord told Jacob that he would be the father of many nations and that the promised land would belong to him and his descendants. Jacob, or Israel, had twelve sons. Their families are known as the twelve tribes of Israel.

Israel had special feelings of love for his son Joseph. Israel made a coat of many colors for him. Joseph's older brothers were jealous and angry with him. To make matters worse, Joseph had two dreams that made his brothers dislike him even more. In the first dream, Joseph and his brothers were harvesting grain. They each had a bundle of grain, but the brothers' bundles all bowed down to Joseph's bundle. In the second dream, the sun, the moon, and eleven stars (perhaps representing Joseph's eleven brothers) all bowed down to him.

Joseph's older brothers did not want him to rule over them. One day, the brothers took their flocks to a far-off place to feed and water them. Israel sent Joseph to see how the brothers were doing. When they saw Joseph coming, some of the brothers made a plan to kill him. But Reuben, the oldest brother, stopped them. He said that, instead of killing him, they should put Joseph in a pit.

When Joseph reached his brothers, they took the colorful coat off his back and threw Joseph into a deep pit. They had planned to leave him there, but some spice merchants on camels rode by on their way to Egypt. Judah talked the other brothers into selling Joseph to the merchants. They sold Joseph for twenty pieces of silver.

The brothers then killed a goat, put the goat's blood on Joseph's coat, and took the coat to their father. When he saw it, Israel cried out, thinking that an evil beast had devoured his son. Israel mourned for Joseph for many days.

Patriarchal Blessings

Every member of the Church belongs to one of the twelve tribes of Israel. When we receive a patriarchal blessing, we learn to which of the twelve tribes we belong. When we enter into the covenant of baptism and join the Church, we may receive all the blessings promised to Abraham, Isaac, and Jacob ("About Patriarchal Blessings," 32).

Joseph in Egypt

Egypt

Egypt is the country southwest of Canaan. The Nile, the longest river in the world, runs through the center of Egypt, enabling many crops to grow there.

Pharaoh

The pharaoh was the king of Egypt, and the people thought of him as a god (Holzapfel et al., *World,* 74).

Dreams

Sometimes God communicates with His children through dreams (Bible Dictionary, 659).

More Than Twenty Years

Joseph was seventeen years old when he was sold into Egypt. He had been a slave or prisoner for thirteen years and was thirty years old when he was brought before Pharaoh. Added to that number were Egypt's seven years of plenty and several years of famine before Joseph's brothers traveled to Egypt for food.

In Egypt, the merchants who bought Joseph from his brothers sold him to Potiphar, the captain of Pharaoh's guard. Joseph served Potiphar well, and the Lord was with him. Potiphar trusted Joseph and put him in charge of his household and possessions.

Potiphar's wife was a wicked woman. She tried to get Joseph to kiss her, but Joseph knew he shouldn't. He ran away, leaving a piece of clothing in her hand. Potiphar's wife told the men of the house that Joseph had attacked her. She showed them the piece of clothing Joseph had left behind. Potiphar believed his wife's lies, and he put Joseph in prison.

Even in prison, the Lord blessed Joseph. The king's butler and baker were in the same prison. One morning, they were worried about dreams they had had. Joseph told them that the Lord would help him explain what the dreams meant.

The butler dreamed of a vine with three branches and three clusters of grapes. In the dream, the butler gave juice from the grapes to Pharaoh. Joseph said that in three days the butler would serve Pharaoh as he had done before. The baker dreamed that birds were eating food from three baskets on his head. Joseph explained that in three days the king would hang the baker from a tree.

Three days later, everything happened just as Joseph said it would. Joseph had asked the butler to tell Pharaoh about him, but the butler forgot. Joseph spent two more years in prison.

One night, Pharaoh had two dreams. First, he dreamed that seven skinny cows swallowed up seven fat cows. In the second dream, seven thin ears of corn swallowed up seven good ears. The Egyptian wise men could not explain the dreams. Suddenly, Pharaoh's butler remembered Joseph in prison, and Pharaoh sent for him. God helped Joseph understand the dreams. Both dreams had the same meaning: There would be seven years with plenty of food in Egypt, followed by seven years of famine.

Pharaoh saw that God was with Joseph. He released Joseph from prison and gave him charge over all the land. Joseph directed the Egyptians to grow and store food for seven years. After the years of plenty, the earth became so dry that nothing would grow. People in other lands were starving, but because the Egyptians had followed Joseph's directions, they had enough to eat.

In Canaan, where Joseph's family lived, food was scarce. Joseph's father sent his sons to Egypt to buy food. The youngest, Benjamin, stayed home.

When the ten brothers arrived in Egypt, it had been more than twenty years since they had seen Joseph. They did not recognize him, and he didn't tell them who he was. Instead, he accused them of being spies and put them in prison. After three days, he sold them the grain they needed and sent them back to Canaan to get their youngest brother. When they returned with Benjamin, Joseph invited them to eat at his home. The brothers still did not know who he was. Joseph wept when he saw Benjamin and fed him well. Joseph ordered his men to fill the brothers' sacks with grain, put their money back in their sacks— and put Joseph's own silver cup in Benjamin's sack.

On their way back to Canaan, Joseph's steward caught up with the brothers. Finding the cup in Benjamin's sack, he arrested them and brought them back to Joseph. The brothers bowed down to Joseph and begged him to release Benjamin, knowing how sad their father would be to lose his youngest son. When Judah offered to stay in Benjamin's place, Joseph saw how they cared for Benjamin, and he could not keep from weeping. He ordered everyone to leave the room except his brothers, and at last he told them who he was. Joseph held Benjamin close and wept. He kissed all of his brothers and told them not to be angry with themselves for what they had done to him. He assured them that God had been with him and had prepared a way for Joseph to save his family. Joseph forgave his brothers and invited them to move their father and their families to Egypt.

The Baby Moses

Bricks from Clay

Making bricks was hard work for the Israelite slaves. They worked in the sun all day mixing mud with straw, putting the mud into molds, and letting the bricks harden before they could be used for building (Holzapfel et al., *World,* 82).

After the family of Jacob (or Israel, as he came to be called) moved to Egypt, they had many children, grandchildren, and great-grandchildren. Before long, the land was filled with Israelites.

The new king, or pharaoh, who ruled Egypt did not know Joseph and his family. He feared that the Israelites would outnumber and become mightier than the Egyptians. Pharaoh even thought the Israelites might join Egypt's enemies and fight against Egypt. He put taskmasters over the Israelites and made them slaves. They worked hard all day, making bricks from mud, laboring in the fields, and building treasure cities for Pharaoh.

Even though their lives became bitter with hard bondage, the Israelites continued to thrive. Eventually, Pharaoh ordered the midwives, or the nurses who helped deliver babies, to kill every newborn baby boy. The midwives loved God more than they feared Pharaoh, so they did not kill the babies, and the Lord blessed them for their righteousness.

When Pharaoh realized that the midwives were not doing as he asked, he commanded that the baby boys be thrown into the river. About this time, an Israelite woman gave birth to a boy who would later be named Moses. Worried that the Egyptians would find out about him, she hid the baby for three months, until she felt he could no longer be hidden. The loving mother made a small ark, or basket, of bulrushes, laid the baby in the basket in the river, and told his older sister, Miriam, to watch over him.

Miriam watched as the basket floated to the place on the riverbank where the daughter of Pharaoh was washing herself. The princess sent her maid to fetch the ark. When the princess opened the basket, the baby cried. The princess had compassion on the baby even though she knew he was an Israelite. When Miriam came forward and offered to find an Israelite woman to nurse the baby, Pharaoh's daughter agreed. The baby's own mother took care of him until it was time to take him back to live with the princess.

Pharaoh's daughter named the baby Moses and raised him as her son. He was taught and became learned in all the ways of the Egyptians. Moses grew to be a great leader who ultimately led the Israelites to freedom.

Miriam

Miriam was Moses' older sister, who risked her life to watch over him as a baby in the basket. She grew to be an Israelite leader with prophetic gifts.

The Prophet Moses

The Ten Plagues

1. Water from the Nile River is turned to blood.

2. Frogs from the Nile infest the Egyptians' land and homes.

3. Dust becomes lice (wingless insects) and infects people, animals, and property.

4. Flies swarm the land.

5. Egyptians' cattle suddenly die.

6. Boils and blains (open sores) infect the Egyptians and their animals.

7. Hail and fire fall everywhere except where the Israelites live.

While saving the life of an Israelite, Prince Moses slew an Egyptian. Knowing that Pharaoh would kill him for what he had done, Moses fled Egypt and found safety in Midian with a priest named Jethro. Moses married Zipporah, one of Jethro's seven daughters, and lived peacefully as a shepherd.

One day while he was herding sheep, Moses saw a bush on the mountain that was burning but was not consumed by the fire. When he took a closer look at the miraculous bush, he heard the Lord's voice calling his name. Moses answered, "Here am I." The Lord instructed Moses to return to Egypt and free his people, the Israelites, from slavery. When Moses asked how it would be possible for him to do such a thing, the Lord told him that He would be with him. Moses wondered how he, being slow of speech, could speak to the people. The Lord reassured Moses that He would send Moses' brother, Aaron, to be a spokesman for him. Aaron went to Moses in the wilderness, and together they traveled to Egypt.

Moses and Aaron went to Pharaoh's court and told him that the Lord had commanded him to set their people free. Pharaoh's heart was hard, and he said, "Who is the Lord, that I should obey his voice to let Israel go?" Pharaoh then decreed that the Israelite slaves must work harder. Moses and Aaron showed Pharaoh that the Lord was more powerful than he was. Moses threw his staff to the ground, and by the power of God it turned into a serpent. Pharaoh told them that his magicians could perform such a "trick." But when they did, Moses' rod swallowed up the magicians' rods.

The next morning, Moses and Aaron met Pharaoh by the river's edge and again asked him to free the Israelites. When Pharaoh refused, Moses struck the river with his rod. The river was turned to blood, and the fish died. By the power of God, all the water in Egypt, even the water that people had stored in pots, turned to blood. But Pharaoh's heart was still hard. Through the power of God, Moses and Aaron caused that frogs, lice, and then flies should infest the land. But Pharaoh still would not set the Israelites free. All of the Egyptians' cattle died, and the Israelites' cattle did not, but Pharaoh still would not acknowledge the hand of God. The Egyptians were smitten with boils, blains, locusts, and hail mixed with fire—and yet, Pharaoh would not bow to the God of Israel and set the people free.

Moses stretched forth his hand and caused darkness to cover the land for three days. It was dark throughout Egypt—but not inside the Israelites' homes. Even in the darkness, Pharaoh's heart was hard. Moses then gave the people a warning from the Lord: At midnight, every firstborn child and animal in Egypt would grow sick and die. But the Israelites would be saved if they put the blood of a lamb on the posts beside and above their doors. The Israelites obeyed, and the lives of their firstborn were saved, but all of the Egyptians—even the pharaoh—lost their firstborn children and animals.

At last, Pharaoh acknowledged the power of Israel's God, and he set the Israelites free.

8. Locusts (a kind of grasshopper) invade the land.

9. Thick darkness covers the land for three days.

10. The firstborn of man and beast die.

The Israelites Leave Egypt

The Passover

Death "passed over" the Israelites who put lamb's blood on their upper and side doorposts, but all of the Egyptian firstborn died. Jewish people still remember this event with a holiday and a feast.

Just after midnight, a great cry of mourning went throughout Egypt. Moses had warned Pharaoh that if he did not obey God and set the Israelites free, every firstborn child and animal in Egypt would become sick and die. It happened just as Moses said it would, and now Pharaoh feared that all Egyptians might die. During the middle of the night, Pharaoh called for Moses and Aaron and told them to take their people and leave Egypt.

After 430 years of slavery to the Egyptians, the Israelites were finally set free! At least six hundred thousand Israelite men, along with women and children, quickly gathered their families, their animals, and their belongings. They did not even wait for their bread dough to rise. They borrowed what they needed from the Egyptians, and they left.

The Lord told Moses to lead the people through the wilderness toward the Red Sea. He showed them where to go by sending a cloud to guide

their way by day and a pillar of fire to light their way by night. The Lord told Moses to have the people camp by the Red Sea.

A short while after the Israelites left Egypt, Pharaoh and the Egyptians began to ask themselves why they had let the Israelites go. Now who would be their servants? Pharaoh readied his chariot and his army and chased after the Israelites.

When the Israelites saw the Egyptians approaching, they were afraid. Moses told them not to fear. He reminded them that the Lord would fight for them. The cloud and pillar of fire that had gone before the Israelites now stood behind them, so the Egyptians could not come near them during the night. Moses stretched his rod over the Red Sea, and the Lord caused a strong wind to blow all through the night. The waters of the sea were blown back and divided, and a way was opened for the Israelites to walk through on dry ground. They passed through the Red Sea with walls of water on their right and on their left.

The next morning, the Egyptians tried to follow the Israelites into the passageway. The Lord told Moses to lift his hand over the sea—and the walls of water crashed down on Pharaoh's soldiers, chariots, and horses. All of the Egyptian host who had come into the passageway were swallowed up and drowned.

The Israelites realized that the Lord had saved their lives. They offered prayers of praise and gratitude, and they sang and danced to show God how thankful they felt. Moses' sister, Miriam, danced and shook a timbrel, or ancient tambourine, as she sang her song of gratitude to the Lord.

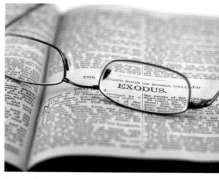

Exodus

Exodus is a Greek word meaning "departure." Exodus is the name of the book in the Bible that relates how the Israelites departed from Egypt.

The Israelites in the Wilderness

The Ten Commandments

1. Thou shalt have no other gods before me.
2. Thou shalt not make unto thee any graven image.
3. Thou shalt not take the name of the Lord thy God in vain.
4. Remember the Sabbath day, to keep it holy.
5. Honor thy father and thy mother.
6. Thou shalt not kill.
7. Thou shalt not commit adultery.
8. Thou shalt not steal.
9. Thou shalt not bear false witness against thy neighbor.
10. Thou shalt not covet.

Three days after the Israelites' escape through the Red Sea, they began to be thirsty. The water they found was too bitter to drink. The Lord showed Moses a tree to throw into the water, and the water became sweet to drink.

Soon there was not enough food to eat, and the people murmured that they should have stayed in Egypt. The Lord promised to rain down food from heaven. That evening, He sent quails into their camp for the Israelites to eat, and in the morning they found sweet, white flakes that had fallen like dew on the ground. They called the food *manna*. The Lord instructed the people to gather as much manna as they needed for one day and no more. If they gathered more, the next morning the day-old manna would smell bad and be full of worms. But on the sixth day of the week, they were allowed to gather enough food for two days so they could rest on the Sabbath. Only on the Sabbath did the manna remain good to eat the second day. The Lord fed the Israelites with manna for forty years.

As they journeyed on, once again they could not find water. The people were so angry that they were almost ready to throw stones at Moses. The Lord told him to strike a large rock with his rod. When Moses smote the rock, water flowed out of it, and the people had all they needed.

A man named Amalek led an army against the Israelites. Moses stood on top of a hill, holding up the rod of God. When the rod was held high, Israel triumphed in the battle. If Moses let his arms down, Amalek prevailed. Moses' arms became tired, and Aaron and a man named Hur held up Moses' arms for him until the sun went down and the Israelites won the battle.

The Lord told Moses to write about these miracles so the people would always remember them.

Two months after leaving Egypt, the Israelites arrived at Mount Sinai. Moses went up the mount, and there the Lord told him to prepare the people to receive God's laws. Moses instructed the people to wash their clothing and repent of their sins so they would be ready to hear the word of the Lord. The morning of the third day, thunder, lightning, and a thick cloud were seen on Mount Sinai. A trumpet sounded so loudly that the people in the camp trembled.

Moses brought the people to the foot of the mountain. He told them not to go up into Mount Sinai or even to touch the mountain or they would die. The glory of the Lord filled the mount, and it appeared to be covered with smoke. The ground shook, and the trumpet sounded louder and louder. Then Moses spoke, and the people heard the voice of God. The Lord gave Moses and the people the Ten Commandments. Moses told the people all the words of the Lord, and they promised to obey.

As God commanded, Moses again went up the mount, with his brother Aaron, Aaron's sons, and seventy of the elders of Israel. They saw the Lord there, standing on a beautiful pavement of sapphire. The Lord called Moses to go higher up the mount to receive more instruction. The others returned to the camp, and Moses stayed on Mount Sinai, fasting for forty days and nights. The Lord talked with him and, with His own finger, wrote the commandments on stone tablets.

Tired of waiting for Moses to come down from the mountain, the worried Israelites begged Aaron to make an idol for them to worship. They gave him their gold jewelry, which he melted and shaped into a golden calf. The people brought sacrifices and worshipped the calf.

Moses came down from the mountain and saw the people singing and dancing around the idol, some of them wearing no clothing. Moses threw down the stone tablets, breaking them in pieces. He tore down the golden calf and ground it to powder. Moses angrily told his brother and the Israelites that they must repent of this great sin. He asked, "Who is on the Lord's side?" At the Lord's command, many wicked Israelites died that day.

The Lord told Moses to cut two new stone tablets and return to the mount. Moses spoke with the Lord face to face, and the Lord again wrote His commandments on the stone tablets. When Moses returned to the camp, his face was so filled with light that the Israelites were afraid to look at him. Moses placed a veil over his face, gathered the people, and gave them the laws of God.

Manna

Manna looked like white coriander seed and tasted like thin cakes made with honey. It could be ground into flour to make a kind of bread or cake. Each person gathered about an omer, or approximately half a gallon, of manna every day.

How Many Israelites?

The Bible records that there were six hundred thousand men over the age of twenty who followed Moses out of Egypt. Adding women and children, the total could have been more than two million people (OT student manual 1:119). Some scholars believe the numbers should be lower (Holzapfel et al., *World,* 126).

The Tabernacle

The Ark of the Covenant

The Lord told Moses to build a wooden chest, cover it with gold, and place the stone tablets inside. The Israelites carried the ark with them wherever they went, and its usual resting place was in the Holy of Holies.

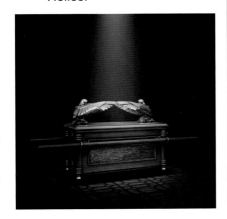

During their journey in the wilderness, the Lord commanded the Israelites to build a tabernacle, or portable temple, where the Lord might visit his people. He told them exactly what materials to use and how tall and wide the tabernacle should be. It was like a large tent surrounded by a courtyard, and it was divided into three parts: the outer courtyard and two rooms inside the tent—the Holy Place and the Holy of Holies. There was a veil between the Holy Place and the Holy of Holies. A cloud rested above the tabernacle during the day, and fire rested above it at night. These signs showed the people that God was with them. The Israelites lived by Mount Sinai for a year, worshipping God in the tabernacle.

When the cloud of the Lord was taken up and no longer rested on the tabernacle, the Israelites followed the cloud and journeyed into the wilderness. Even though they knew the Lord was leading them, they again began to complain. They were tired of eating manna. Forgetting that it was the Lord who had blessed them with food, they said they wanted to eat fish, fruits, and vegetables like they had in Egypt.

Dimensions of the Tabernacle

The tent of the tabernacle was 30 cubits long by 10 cubits wide (one cubit is the distance from the elbow to the fingertip, or about 18 to 22 inches), or roughly the size of the Primary room in some of our Church buildings today (OT student manual 1:147–48).

Moses prayed to the Lord for strength and help to meet the people's needs. The Lord commanded Moses to bring seventy of the elders of Israel to the tabernacle, where He would visit them and bless them with His spirit. When the seventy elders gathered around the tabernacle, the Lord came down in a cloud, and His Spirit rested upon them. From that time on, the elders prophesied, and they shared with Moses the burden of leading the people.

Two men, named Eldad and Medad, who were in the camp but not in the tabernacle with the others, also felt the Lord's Spirit and began to prophesy. When a young man ran and told Moses that Eldad and Medad were prophesying in the camp, Joshua thought Moses should make them stop. But Moses replied that he wished that all of the Lord's people could prophesy and have the Holy Ghost with them. Even though not everyone could be inside the tabernacle, the Lord's prophet wanted all of them to be able to feel His Spirit and receive His strength.

Joshua and the Battle of Jericho

The Promised Land

Also known as Canaan, the promised land was much more fertile than the surrounding deserts. It had everything the Israelites would need to grow food to feed themselves and their animals and people (Holzapfel et al., *World*, 135).

The Brazen Serpent

Before the Israelites entered the promised land, fiery serpents invaded their camp and bit many of the people. The Lord told Moses to make a serpent of brass and mount it on a pole. If a person who had been bitten looked at the brass serpent, he or she would not die.

When the Israelites reached Canaan, the Lord told Moses to send a spy from each tribe to survey the land. The spies reported that the land flowed with milk and honey, meaning that food was plentiful there. But, they said, the people were like giants, and the cities had great walls around them. Two of the spies, Caleb and Joshua, were sure that, with the Lord's help, they could conquer the land. But the people were afraid and wanted to go back to Egypt. The Lord was disappointed with the people's lack of faith. He decreed that they should wander in the wilderness for forty years, until those who did not believe had died. Then their children would possess the land.

Moses became an old man. He had led the people of Israel for forty years, and the Lord told him his time on earth would soon end. Moses blessed Joshua and gave him authority to lead the Israelites. He told the people to be strong and courageous and to obey God. When Moses was 120 years old, he climbed to the top of Mount Pisgah. There, the Lord showed him all of the promised land and assured Moses that He would give the land to the Israelites. Then the Lord took Moses to Himself. The people mourned many days for their great prophet.

After Moses was gone, the Lord told Joshua to prepare the people to enter the promised land. Joshua instructed them to gather food and be ready

to leave their camp in three days. He sent two spies to Jericho, the first city they would encounter in the promised land. The spies entered the city and stayed in the home of a woman named Rahab. The king of Jericho learned about the spies and sent his men to Rahab's home. She hid the spies under some stalks of flax on her roof, and the king's men could not find them.

The spies were grateful to Rahab for saving their lives. They promised that she and her family would not be harmed when the Israelites invaded the city. They told her to tie a red cord in her window and take all of her family inside her house. There they would be safe.

A few days later, Joshua led the Israelites to the Jordan River and told them to humble themselves and prepare to receive the Lord's help. Early the next morning, Joshua called the priests to carry the ark of the covenant across the river before the people. The moment the priests set their feet in the Jordan River, the deep water was cut off, and they stood on dry ground. The water stayed back until all the Israelites had crossed to the other side.

When the Canaanites saw that the Lord had helped the Israelites cross the river, they fled to their homes and locked the city gates. Joshua prepared the Israelites to go to battle. Once a day for six days, the army followed priests carrying the ark of the covenant around the city. Seven more priests blew on trumpets made from rams' horns. On the seventh day, the priests and the army circled the city seven times. When the priests blew one final blast on the trumpets, the Israelites shouted—and the walls of Jericho came tumbling down! The Israelites invaded the city, and only Rahab and her family were saved. The Israelites entered the land that had been promised to them for so many years.

Flax on the Roof

Flax is a plant that was often woven to make linen cloth. The plant stalks were placed in water to separate the fibers and then dried on rooftops (Hastings, *Children's,* 93).

Twelve Stones

After the Israelites crossed the Jordan River, Joshua called twelve men, one from each tribe, to carry stones from the river on their shoulders and build a memorial of this event. In later years, when their children asked what the stone memorial meant, the parents would remember and tell them about the miracle of the river crossing.

Samson

Nazarite

Under the law of Moses, some of the people made special promises with God to separate themselves from the world. These people were called Nazarites. One of their promises was never to let a razor come upon their heads, meaning they would not cut their hair or shave their beards (Bible Dictionary, 737; Holzapfel et al., *World,* 128).

An Israelite man named Manoah and his wife were not able to have children. Then an angel appeared to Manoah's wife and told her that she was going to give birth to a son. The angel told the woman she must not drink wine or any strong drink or eat anything unclean because her son's life would be dedicated to God. As a sign of his devotion, his hair should never be cut and his beard should never be shaved. The angel also told the woman that her son would help to free the Israelites from the hands of their enemies, the Philistines.

Manoah's wife told her husband what had happened, and he prayed that the angel would come again and teach them how to raise this child. The Lord heard Manoah's prayer, and one day while Manoah's wife was sitting in the field, the angel appeared to her again. The woman ran to get Manoah, and when they returned, the angel spoke to them.

As the angel foretold, Manoah's wife gave birth to a son, and they named him Samson. The spirit of the Lord was with Samson, and he grew to be a very

strong man. He was so strong that he killed a lion with his bare hands. He removed the doors of a city gate, posts and all, and carried them away over his shoulder. And when he was fighting the Philistines, Samson slew a thousand men with only a donkey's jawbone as a weapon.

The Philistines feared Samson. More than anything, they wanted to know the secret of his great strength. When they learned that Samson had fallen in love with a Philistine woman named Delilah, they offered to pay her eleven hundred pieces of silver if she could discover Samson's secret. But Samson only teased her. He told her that if she tied him with seven fresh bowstrings or with new ropes, or if she wove his hair into her loom, he would become weak. But each time Delilah tried these tricks, Samson was as strong as ever.

Delilah became frustrated. She told Samson that if he loved her, he would share his secret with her. Thinking that Delilah loved him and that he could trust her, Samson finally told her the truth: if his hair were cut, he would lose his strength. Later, when Samson fell asleep, Delilah summoned a man to come and shave Samson's head. When Samson awoke, the Philistines captured him, blinded him, and put him in prison. Samson was no longer the strong servant of God he had once been.

While he was in prison, Samson's hair began to grow back. Sometimes the Philistines brought him out to make fun of him. One such time, thousands of people had gathered together in a large building. They called for Samson and placed him between two pillars that held up the roof of the building. When the people laughed at him, Samson prayed to have his strength return to him one last time. He leaned forward and pushed the pillars with all his might—and the roof came tumbling down. Samson and everyone else in the building died.

Philistines

Philistine soldiers, like those who captured Samson, wore feathered head-dresses that made them look tall and fearsome in battle (Hastings, *Children's*, 103).

Ruth and Naomi

In the days when judges ruled Israel, a famine came upon the land, and there was not enough food to eat. A man named Elimelech, his wife, Naomi, and their two sons moved to Moab to find food. They lived in Moab for ten years, and each of the sons married a Moabite woman. The wife of one son was named Orpah, and the wife of the other son was named Ruth. While they lived in Moab, Elimelech died, and sometime later, both of his and Naomi's sons died, too.

Naomi wanted to return to her hometown of Bethlehem. Her daughters-in-law, Orpah and Ruth, started to go with her, but Naomi told them to stay in Moab with their families. Orpah wept and kissed Naomi good-bye, but Ruth clung faithfully to her mother-in-law and and begged to stay with her. Ruth told Naomi that she would go wherever Naomi went and live wherever she lived. Ruth wanted to be with Naomi and her family and worship God in the same way they did.

Naomi and Ruth went to Bethlehem together. Ruth gleaned in the barley and wheat fields to find food for them to eat. A good landowner named Boaz noticed Ruth and welcomed her to glean in his fields. He was impressed with the way she took such good care of Naomi, even leaving her homeland so her

Moabites

Moabites lived in Moab, a land that had been enemy territory to the Israelites for many years. The need to move to Moab shows that Naomi's family were desperate for food (Holzapfel et al., *World,* 185).

Gleaning

Harvesting barley or wheat was hard work. Workers cut through the stalks of grain with sickles—sharp, curved tools—and gathered the grain into bundles called sheaves. The sheaves were then carried away to be stored or used. If any of the grain fell to the ground and was not bound into sheaves, poor people were allowed to come and glean, or gather it up (OT student manual 1:262–63).

mother-in-law would not be left alone. Boaz praised Ruth for her goodness and faith and told her that she would be blessed for trusting God to help her.

One night, Naomi told Ruth to wash and prepare herself to go to the threshing floor to speak to Boaz. That evening, Boaz told Ruth that he knew she was a virtuous woman, or that she was good and faithful, and he wanted to marry her. According to the Israelite custom, Boaz bought Elimelech's land so he could marry Ruth. Naomi was very happy for her faithful daughter-in-law.

After Ruth and Boaz were married, Ruth gave birth to a son. They named him Obed, and Naomi helped care for him. Obed grew to be a man and eventually became the grandfather of King David. Many years later, Jesus Christ was born through this family.

Hannah and Samuel

The Ark of the Covenant Captured

Thinking the ark of the covenant would give them power over the Philistines, the Israelites took it with them to battle. But the Philistines captured the ark and placed it in front of one of their idols. The next night, the idol fell over and broke, and the Philistines were struck with a plague and an infestation of mice. The Philistines were afraid and returned the ark to the Israelites.

Every year, a man named Elkanah and his wife Hannah journeyed to the house of the Lord to worship and to offer sacrifices. One year, Hannah was so sad that she could not even eat. Elkanah loved her dearly and asked her why she was crying. She told him she was sad because she had not been able to have children.

In the temple, Hannah poured out her heart to God. She prayed and wept, and she promised God that if he would bless her with a son, she would give him to the Lord all the days of his life. Eli, the priest who served in the temple, noticed Hannah and talked with her. He told her to return to her home in peace, and he blessed her that God would grant what she had asked of Him.

Hannah returned home, and the Lord remembered her. In time, Hannah gave birth to a son, and she knew the Lord had heard her prayer. She and Elkanah named their son Samuel, which means "heard of God."

Hannah kept her promise to the Lord. When Samuel was about three years old, she took him to the temple to live there and learn to serve God. The priest, Eli, took care of Samuel and trained him well. Each year, when Elkanah and Hannah went to the temple to make sacrifices, Hannah took Samuel a new coat she had made for him. Eli blessed Elkanah and Hannah for their unselfishness, and in time, Hannah gave birth to three more sons and two daughters.

The child Samuel grew while serving with Eli in the temple. One night, Eli had fallen asleep and Samuel had gone to bed. Samuel heard someone call his name, and he answered, "Here I am." Samuel ran to see if Eli had called him, but Eli had not, and he told Samuel to go back to sleep. Three times that night, Samuel heard someone call his name, and each time he ran to Eli and said, "Here I am." Finally, Eli understood. He explained to Samuel that it was the Lord who was calling him. Eli told Samuel to say, "Speak, Lord, for thy servant heareth." The next time the Lord called, this was Samuel's answer, and the Lord spoke with him.

The next morning, Eli asked Samuel what the Lord had said to him. Samuel told Eli everything the Lord had told him. The Lord was preparing Samuel to become a great prophet.

Eli and His Sons

Eli had two sons, Hophni and Phinehas. They chose not to follow God and became very wicked. They were killed in a battle against the Philistines. When Eli heard that the ark of the covenant had been captured and that his sons had died, he fell over backwards from his seat. His neck was broken, and he died.

David and Goliath

Lions

Anciently, Asiatic lions were seen in Israel. Because of their strength and power, lions were sometimes used as a symbol for Jesus Christ (Holzapfel et al., *World,* 201).

For a long time, the prophet Samuel felt sad because Saul, the king of the Israelites, chose to disobey God. Finally, the Lord told Samuel he should not mourn for Saul any longer and that it was time to prepare a new king. He told Samuel to look for the new king among the sons of Jesse, a good man who lived in Bethlehem. Samuel went to Jesse's home, and, one by one, the prophet greeted Jesse's sons. At first, Samuel thought the oldest son, who was large and tall, might be a good king, but the Lord taught Samuel that a person's outward appearance is not as important as what his heart is like. Samuel met seven of Jesse's sons, but the Lord told him that none of these men was the chosen king.

Samuel asked Jesse if he had another son, and Jesse said that his youngest son, David, was tending the sheep. Samuel asked to meet him. When the prophet met David, he knew that David was the one the Lord had chosen to be the next king. Samuel took his horn of oil, poured some of the oil on David's head, and gave him a blessing.

King Saul continued to disobey God and no longer felt the Lord's Spirit. He began to be troubled by an evil feeling. Saul was told about a valiant young man named David, a shepherd who could play the harp well. Whenever he felt anxious or upset, Saul sent for David, whose beautiful music helped the king feel more peaceful. Saul was so pleased with David that he asked him to be his armor bearer.

The Philistines challenged Saul and his army to battle. The Philistines stood on a mountain on one side of a great valley, and Saul and the Israelites stood on a mountain on the other side. Every day for forty days, the Philistines brought out a giant named Goliath, who challenged the Israelites to send someone to fight him. Goliath shouted that if anyone could slay him, the Philistines would become servants to the Israelites.

One day, when David went to the battlefield to take food to his brothers, he heard Goliath shout his challenge to the Israelites. David declared that he would fight the giant. His older brothers tried to discourage him, and King Saul reminded David that he was young and inexperienced. But David told Saul that he had killed a lion and a bear while tending his father's sheep—and that he had faith that the Lord would help him.

Saul gave David permission to fight the giant and equipped him with heavy armor. David was not used to wearing armor, and he took it off. He walked onto the battlefield with no other weapon than his slingshot and five smooth stones. David confronted the giant, saying, "Thou comest to me with a sword, and with a spear, and with a shield: but I come to thee in the name of the Lord of hosts." David put a stone in his sling, swung it around, and let the stone fly. It hit Goliath in the forehead, and he fell to the ground. David grabbed the giant's sword, stood on top of him, and cut off his head. David knew the Lord had helped him slay the giant.

Goliath

Goliath was "six cubits and a span"—or about 9 feet 9 inches tall (OT student manual 1:278).

David and Jonathan

After David slew Goliath, King Saul invited David to live in the palace with his family. David became best friends with the king's son Jonathan. Jonathan loved David so much that he gave him his robe, sword, bow, and belt to wear. Jonathan's sister Michal fell in love with David. David loved her, too, and asked the king if he could marry her, even though he was only a shepherd's son. Saul told David he could marry Michal if he first slew a hundred Philistines in battle. David slew not one hundred but two hundred Philistines, and he married Michal.

King Saul put David in charge of his armies, and David was a wise leader. When David returned from battle, women came out of the cities, singing, "Saul hath slain his thousands, and David his ten thousands." When Saul heard their song and saw how the people admired David, he became jealous.

David Spared Saul's Life on Two Occasions

1. When David was hiding in a cave, King Saul entered the same cave and fell asleep. While Saul was sleeping, David cut off a piece of the king's robe, but he refused to kill him.

2. David found King Saul asleep one night in a trench on the battlefield. David took Saul's spear and waterskin to show Saul that he had been close enough to kill him, but he had spared the king's life.

On these two occasions, David could have killed Saul, but each time he chose to let him live. The king admitted that David was more righteous than he.

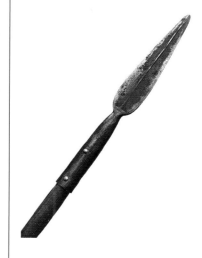

King Saul was so jealous that he tried to kill David. Once, while David was playing the harp for Saul, the king threw his spear at him. But David moved just in time, and the spear stuck in the wall. King Saul put David on the front lines of battle, hoping he would be killed by a Philistine, but it was David who triumphed. One night, King Saul sent servants to David's house to kill him, but Michal helped him escape through a back window. When the king's servants entered David's room, it looked like he was asleep because Michal put an idol and a pillow in the bed where David would have been. David fled and found safety with Samuel the prophet.

When David returned, he met with Jonathan and asked him if it were safe for him to be near the king. Jonathan promised to learn the answer at a feast he would be attending the next day. He and David decided to meet after the feast. At the appointed time, Jonathan came with his servant and shot some arrows beyond where his servant was standing. David knew this was a signal that the king was still angry and that David must go far away. When the servant had gone back to the house, Jonathan and David embraced one last time. They wept as they promised always to be friends and to look after each other's families.

David found safety for a time with a priest, but when Saul learned that the priest had helped David, the priest was killed. Saul spent the rest of his life trying to find and kill David. After some time, during a battle with the Philistines, Saul's three sons, including Jonathan, were killed, and Saul was so badly wounded that he purposely fell on his sword and took his own life. David became the new king of Israel.

Abigail

Baking Bread

To bake their bread, Abigail and her servants probably used outdoor brick ovens fueled by a wood fire (Olson, *Women,* 205).

For ten years, David fled from King Saul and his army. During a part of this time, David hid in the hill country of Judea. He and his army of about six hundred men camped near land owned by an ill-tempered and selfish man named Nabal. David and his army helped protect Nabal's sheep and were friendly to his sheepherders, but Nabal did nothing for them in return. When it came time to shear the sheep, traditionally a time of feasting, David sent ten young men to ask Nabal if David and his men could join the celebration.

Nabal refused to welcome David and his men. He even rudely asked, "Who is David?" According to the ancient custom, not welcoming someone was considered to be especially bad manners. It also defied God's law to love strangers as if they were their own people.

David was very angry at Nabal's refusal, and he rallied four hundred of his men to fight Nabal. While they marched toward Nabal's home, one of the young men who worked for him quickly met with Nabal's beautiful wife, Abigail. The young man told Abigail what had happened and that David's men were coming to avenge themselves for Nabal's rudeness.

Abigail was a good and wise woman. She wanted to obey God and do what was right, so she made a brave decision to welcome David and his men herself. She quickly went to work preparing a feast of two hundred loaves of bread, five sheep, a hundred clusters of raisins, two hundred fig cakes, corn, and all the grape juice the men could drink. She loaded the food on donkeys, mounted her own donkey, and rode down the hill to meet David and his men. When Abigail saw David, she quickly dismounted from her donkey and bowed down before David, pleading for him to forgive Nabal. Abigail's actions softened David's heart, and he called off the attack. He accepted Abigail's gifts and told his men to leave in peace.

The next morning, Abigail told her husband how their lives had been saved when she apologized to David and gave him gifts. After Nabal heard what she had done, he became very ill, and he died ten days later.

David sent his servants to bring Abigail to his home. David saw that Abigail was a woman of great faith who was also very beautiful, and he married her.

Sheepshearing Festival

Usually in the spring, when it was time to shear the wool from the sheep, shepherds held a feast of celebration. At this time, debts were settled and wrongs were pardoned (Olson, *Women*, 202).

King David

Walking on the Roof

In ancient times, many homes in the Middle East had flat roofs. People would often go to their roofs in the evening to feel a breeze and find relief from the heat (OT student manual 1:290).

Psalms

The Bible includes a book of 150 psalms, or songs and poems that express devotion to God. David is thought to have written many of these psalms. He was called the "sweet psalmist of Israel" (2 Samuel 23:1). His psalms describe his love for the Lord and his need and desire for forgiveness.

When David was thirty years old, he became king of all Israel. David prayed before and during his battles, and the Lord loved and protected him. He won many battles and became great in the eyes of the people. They greatly admired and respected him.

King David arranged to have the ark of the covenant brought from Shiloh to the capital city of Jerusalem. He wanted to build a house unto the Lord and place the ark there. He counseled with the prophet Nathan about building a temple, but the Lord told David that this was not for him to do. David had fought in too many wars and shed too much blood. The Lord promised David, though, that his son who would come after him would build a temple and that Jesus Christ, the Son of God, would be born through David's family line.

When he became king, David remembered his promise to his dear friend Jonathan, the son of King Saul. Jonathan had died in battle against the Philistines, and David sent his servant to see if any of Jonathan's sons still lived. The servant found Jonathan's son, Mephibosheth, who was disabled—he couldn't walk. David gave Mephibosheth all of the land that Saul's family had once owned. David also invited him to always eat at the king's table. Mephibosheth was amazed that the king would be so kind to him.

One year, instead of doing his duty in going to battle with his men, David stayed home. He was walking on his rooftop one evening when he looked down into another courtyard and saw a beautiful woman washing herself. Instead of turning away, David chose to look at the woman, whose name was Bathsheba. He sent his servant to bring her to him. Even though she was already married, David wanted her for his wife, which was a great sin. Then he committed another sin by sending Bathsheba's husband, Uriah, to fight on the front line of battle, where Uriah was killed. David married Bathsheba, but the Lord was very displeased with him. The prophet Nathan told David that he had greatly sinned. King David reigned for forty years, but for the rest of his life he felt great sorrow for what he had done and pled for forgiveness from the Lord.

King Solomon

Dimensions of the Temple of Solomon

The temple was long and narrow, about 100 feet long and 30 feet wide. Chambers, or rooms, were built around the outside of the temple building, but the inner structure was exactly twice the size of the tabernacle in the wilderness (Talmage, *House,* 6).

When David was very old, his wife Bathsheba and the prophet Nathan asked him who should be king after he died. One of David's sons, Adonijah, was already preparing to take over the kingdom. David told Bathsheba and Nathan that the Lord wanted his son Solomon to be king. Nathan and the priest Zadok told Solomon to ride King David's mule into the city, where all the people could see him. Zadok took a horn of holy anointing oil from the tabernacle and, pouring a small amount of oil on Solomon's head, anointed him king of Israel. The people blew their trumpets and pipes, rejoicing for their new king. David admonished Solomon to keep the commandments and follow the Lord, and then King David died.

Solomon wanted to be a good and righteous king. One night he had a dream in which the Lord appeared to him. The Lord told Solomon He would give him whatever he desired. Solomon could have asked for anything, but his request was that the Lord give him a wise and understanding heart so that he would be able to judge the people in righteousness. The Lord was pleased with Solomon's desires, and He blessed Solomon with great wisdom.

People sought Solomon's counsel in solving their problems. Two women who lived in the same house came to the king, bringing a baby boy that each of them claimed was her own. One of the women explained that the other woman's baby had died during the night. That woman had taken the living baby away from its true mother. The other woman refused to admit that she had done such a thing. King Solomon showed his wisdom in determining which woman should have the baby. He asked his servant to bring him a sword and said he was going to cut the baby in half and give one half to each woman. When the first woman heard this, she pled with Solomon not to kill the baby. She said she would rather give her baby to the other woman than see this happen to him. Immediately, Solomon knew that this woman must be the true mother, and he gave the baby to her.

Two years after Solomon became king, he began building a beautiful temple, a house of the Lord. Solomon's father, King David, had gathered gold, silver, and all of the best materials to build the temple. Timber and stone came from Solomon's friend Hiram, king of Tyre. Thousands of craftsmen worked seven years to finish the temple. When Solomon dedicated the house to the Lord, a cloud, full of the glory of the Lord, filled the temple. The Lord accepted the house and blessed all who went there to worship.

Queen of Sheba

King Solomon became very famous. The Queen of Sheba traveled many miles to meet him, bringing a great train of camels, spices, gold, and precious stones. The Queen of Sheba was impressed with Solomon's wisdom and prosperity. They exchanged gifts with each other before she returned to her own country (1 Kings 10:1–13).

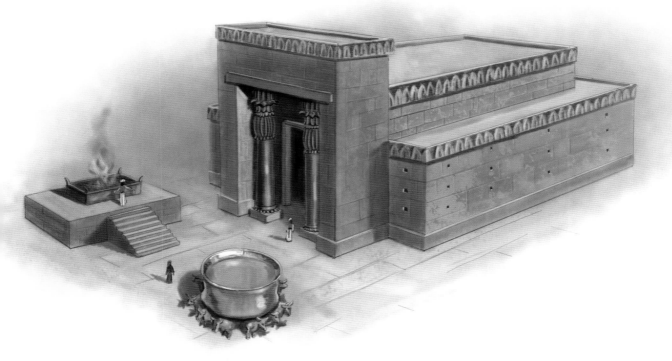

Elijah and the Widow of Zarephath

City Gate

Ancient cities had gates that were closed at night to protect the people from invaders (Olson, *Women*, 226).

Elijah was a prophet during the reign of King Ahab of Israel. Ahab was a wicked king, and he was married to a wicked woman named Jezebel, who was responsible for the deaths of many prophets. When Elijah warned the people that there would be no rain if they did not repent, Jezebel wanted him to be killed, too. The Lord told Elijah to hide from Jezebel.

Elijah did as the Lord commanded. He found a place to hide by a small stream of water. Each morning and evening, the Lord sent ravens with bread and meat for Elijah. He drank water from the stream, but after a while, the lack of rain caused even the stream to dry up.

The Lord sent Elijah to the city of Zarephath, telling him that a certain widow there would feed him. When Elijah came to the city gates, he saw the woman gathering sticks for a fire. Elijah called to her, asking if she would give him some water to drink. As she was going for the water, Elijah asked her if she would bring him some bread, too. She explained

Zarephath

Zarephath, now in the country called Lebanon, was a small town near the ocean. It was also the wicked queen Jezebel's hometown (Valetta et al., *Families,* 323).

The Kingdom of Israel and the Kingdom of Judah

After Solomon's reign, the kingdom of Israel was divided. The ten northern tribes still called themselves the kingdom of Israel, but they soon began worshipping idols. The two tribes in the south were known as the kingdom of Judah, with Jerusalem as their capital city. This kingdom's people became known as Jews (Bible Dictionary, 708).

that she did not have enough bread even for herself and her son to eat. She told Elijah that she had only a handful of meal and a little oil left. She had planned to make a fire and cook what she had for her and her son to eat, and then they would die. Elijah told her not to be afraid. He promised her that if she would feed him first, the Lord would bless her with meal in her barrel and oil in her jar until the drought ended and the Lord sent rain.

The widow of Zarephath had great faith. She prepared a small cake for Elijah, giving away the last of her food. And when she looked in her barrel, she miraculously found more meal. And when she looked in her jar, she miraculously found more oil. Every day, she was able to feed Elijah, her son, and herself, and every day her supply of food was replenished until the drought ended.

While Elijah was staying with them, the woman's son became very sick and died. The mother mourned greatly for her son. Elijah picked the boy up, carried him into the loft of the house, and laid him on his own bed. Elijah cried to the Lord, stretching himself over the child three times and asking the Lord to let the child live again. The Lord heard his prayer, and the boy came back to life. Elijah took the child to his mother. She thanked him, and she knew once more that Elijah was a man of God.

Elijah and the Prophets of Baal

Elijah and the Sealing Power

Hundreds of years later, when Jesus was on the earth, the prophet Elijah delivered the keys of the priesthood to Peter, James, and John on the Mount of Transfiguration. In 1836, Elijah conferred the sealing power on Joseph Smith and Oliver Cowdery in the Kirtland Temple (Doctrine and Covenants 110:13–16).

After three years without rain, the Lord sent Elijah to tell King Ahab that the drought would soon be over. On his way to see the king, Elijah met Obadiah, the governor of King Ahab's house. Elijah told Obadiah that he wanted to meet with the king.

Upon seeing Elijah, Ahab asked if he were the one who had been "troubling Israel." Elijah declared that it was Ahab himself who had caused trouble for Israel by worshipping false gods and disobeying the commandments. Elijah challenged Ahab to gather his people and his false prophets and meet him on the top of Mount Carmel.

All of the people and 450 prophets of the false god Baal met Elijah on the mountain. Elijah asked the Israelites how long they would waver between following the true God and worshipping false gods, and then he issued a challenge. He explained that two young cattle, or bullocks, had been prepared to offer as sacrifices upon the altar. The god who answered their prayers that day by sending down fire to consume the sacrifices would be recognized as the true God.

The false prophets of Baal spread kindling wood on the altar and placed one of the bullocks on the wood. The prophets prayed all morning to Baal, but nothing happened. In the afternoon, they leaped upon the altar, continued to cry out, and did strange things

to show their devotion to the false god. The whole day passed, but no fire appeared to burn the sacrifice.

In the evening, Elijah invited the people who had been watching the "prophets" of Baal to come closer to the altar. Elijah gathered twelve stones—one for each of the twelve tribes of Israel—and built another altar. He made a trench around it and placed more wood and the other bullock on the altar. Elijah then poured four barrels of water over the sacrifice and the wood. He poured four more barrels of water, and then four more, until water surrounded the altar. He even filled the trench with water. Then Elijah lifted his voice to the Lord, asking Him to show His power so that the people would know He was the true God. Fire from the Lord fell from heaven! It burned the wet wood, the sacrifice, the stones, and even licked up the water in the trench. The people knew Elijah was a true prophet and that his God was the true God. They bowed down and said, "The Lord, he is the God."

God commanded Elijah to destroy all of the false prophets of Baal. Then Elijah told Ahab to prepare for an abundance of rain. The drought was over.

Mount Carmel

Mount Carmel is a relatively small mountain, covered by forests, near the Mediterranean Sea. Because it is so green, it is often used in the scriptures as a symbol of fruitfulness (Holzapfel et al., *World,* 259).

The Prophet Elisha

Translated Beings

Elijah was translated, which means his body was changed and he did not experience death before he was taken to heaven.

Mantle

Elijah's coat, or mantle, was a symbol of his authority as the prophet. When he put his mantle over Elisha's shoulders, Elijah demonstrated that the Lord had called Elisha to be the next prophet (OT student manual 2:62).

When the wicked queen Jezebel heard that Elijah had called down fire from heaven and killed the false prophets with a sword, she wanted to kill him. Elijah fled for his life into the wilderness. After a day's journey, he sat under a juniper tree and wondered if it were his time to die. Elijah fell asleep, and an angel of the Lord awakened him and brought him food and water. After Elijah ate, he fell back to sleep, and the angel woke him and fed him again. The angel explained that Elijah had a long journey ahead of him, and he would need strength. Elijah's work was not finished.

Elijah traveled for forty days and forty nights until he arrived at Mount Sinai. He hid inside a cave on the mountainside. The Lord told Elijah to meet him on the mountain. A great wind began to blow. The wind was so strong that the rocks on the mountain were broken in pieces. But the Lord was not in the wind. An earthquake shook the mountain, but the Lord was not in the earthquake. Then fire erupted! But the Lord was not in the fire. After the fire, Elijah heard a still, small voice—it was the voice of the Lord. He told Elijah to find a man named Elisha, to pour holy oil on Elisha's head, and to anoint him to be the prophet in Elijah's place.

Elijah left the mountain and found Elisha plowing in his father's field. Elijah placed his own mantle, or coat, over Elisha's shoulders as a symbol that Elijah's authority was now being passed to the new prophet. Elisha left his oxen, kissed his parents good-bye, and went with Elijah. For several

years, wherever Elijah went, Elisha followed. At last, one day when they came to the Jordan River, Elijah folded his mantle in his hands and hit the river with it. The river divided, and the prophets walked through on dry ground.

Knowing that his time on earth would soon be over, Elijah asked Elisha what he could do for him. More than anything, Elisha wanted to have the Spirit of the Lord with him. He asked to be blessed with spiritual power and strength. While they were talking, the heavens opened. A chariot and horses of fire swept by and took Elijah to heaven in a whirlwind. Elijah was translated.

Elisha missed his dear friend, Elijah the prophet. Elisha kept Elijah's mantle, and with it, he performed the same miracle Elijah had performed: he touched the river with the mantle, and the waters separated. Elijah walked back across the Jordan River on dry ground. When some righteous young men saw what he had done, they bowed before Elisha and honored him as the new prophet. Elisha became a great and powerful man. He performed mighty miracles in the northern part of Israel, and kings looked to him for guidance and counsel.

The Miracles of Elisha

Floating Axe

Some righteous young men were building a home when one of them dropped an axe head in the river. Elisha threw a stick into the water and the heavy axe head floated to the surface (2 Kings 6:1–7).

For more than fifty years, Elisha served as a prophet in Israel, performing many miracles among the people. One day, a widow went to Elisha for help. She did not have enough money to pay a man what she owed him. The man threatened to take her sons and make them his servants if she did not give him the money. Elisha asked the widow if she had anything she could sell. The widow said that all she had was a jar of oil. Elisha told her to go to her friends and neighbors and borrow every empty jar she could find. The prophet told her to pour oil from her jar into the empty jars. Miraculously, from her one jar of oil, she filled all of the other jars. Elisha told her to sell the oil in the jars. The money she received from selling the oil was enough to pay the man, and the woman and her family had enough for all of their needs.

Elisha often passed through the city of Shunem. A woman and her husband invited him to stay with them. They fed him and made a room for him. The woman and her husband had never been able to have children. When Elisha promised the woman that she would give birth to a son, she could hardly believe him, but about a year later she had a baby boy! One day when the son was older, he went to his father in the fields and told his father that he had a very bad headache. His father told him to go home to his mother. She held him in her arms for several hours before he died. The sad mother quickly mounted a donkey and went to look for Elisha. Finding him on Mount Carmel, she pled with him to come and revive her son. The prophet returned to Shunem with the boy's mother. Elisha prayed to the Lord and stretched himself over the boy. Suddenly, the boy

sneezed seven times and opened his eyes. His mother bowed before Elisha and thanked God for the miracle of her son's life.

Naaman, a leader of the Syrian army, was stricken with leprosy. He had sores all over his body, and his skin was falling off. A little maid who helped Naaman's wife was an Israelite, and she told Naaman's wife that a prophet named Elisha could heal her husband. Naaman first went to the king of Israel to see if he could help him, but the king became frightened because he didn't know what to do. When Elisha heard about Naaman, he sent for him. Naaman went to Elisha's home, and the prophet sent a messenger to tell Naaman to wash in the Jordan River seven times and he would be healed. At first, Naaman was angry that Elisha sent his servant instead of talking to Naaman himself. He also wanted to know why the prophet would tell him to wash in the Jordan River. He thought the rivers in his own country were better than all the waters of Israel. Naaman's servants encouraged him to obey the prophet's words. Naaman humbled himself and washed in the Jordan River seven times. Miraculously, he was healed, and all of the sores disappeared. His skin became as healthy as a little child's, and he was cured of the disease. Naaman knew that Israel's God was the true God.

Unseen Horses and Chariots

Elisha's servant woke one morning to see the Syrian army with numerous horses and chariots surrounding the city. Elisha said, "Fear not: for they that be with *us* are more than they that be with *them*." He prayed that his servant would be able to see with spiritual eyes, and the servant beheld an unseen army of angels, with horses and chariots of fire, surrounding Elisha (2 Kings 6:8–17; emphasis added).

The Prophet Jonah

Nineveh and Tarshish

Nineveh and Tarshish were in opposite directions from each other.

Jonah received a revelation from the Lord to go to the great city of Nineveh and call the people to repentance. Jonah didn't want to do it. Instead of going to Nineveh, he tried to run in the opposite direction. He boarded a ship bound for Tarshish.

On the sea, a great wind began to blow. The storm had such force that the sailors feared the ship would break apart, and they would all die. They started throwing things overboard to keep the ship afloat. They began to pray to their gods to save them.

During the terrible storm, Jonah fell asleep inside the ship. The shipmaster awakened him and asked how he could sleep in such a terrible storm. The shipmaster told Jonah to get up and join the others in praying for their lives. The sailors asked Jonah who he was and where he came from. Jonah admitted that he had tried to run away from the Lord and that the storm was his fault. He told the sailors to throw him overboard, and they would all be saved. But they did not want to be responsible for Jonah's death. They tried with all their might to row back to land, but the storm was too fierce. Finally, they decided they must throw Jonah overboard. As soon as they did, the sea stopped raging.

The Lord had prepared a great fish to swallow Jonah. For three days and three nights, Jonah stayed in the belly of the fish. He felt sorry for rejecting the Lord's call to go to Nineveh. He repented and said he would keep his promises to the Lord.

The Lord heard his cries, and the fish vomited Jonah onto the land. Again, Jonah received a revelation to call the people of Nineveh to repentance. This time, Jonah obeyed. He journeyed to Nineveh and told the people they must repent or in forty days their city would be destroyed. The people listened to what he said. Even the king took off his royal robe and covered himself in sackcloth and ashes to show that he was sorry for all the wrong things he had done. The king commanded that no man or beast should eat or drink and that all should be covered in sackcloth until God turned his anger away from them. All of the people obeyed the king, and they cried mightily to God and repented of all their wickedness.

Their humility pleased the Lord. He told Jonah that the city of Nineveh would not be destroyed, because its people had repented of their sins.

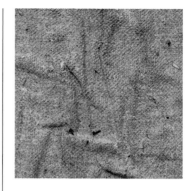

Sackcloth and Ashes

Sackcloth is a rough and uncomfortable fabric that was worn to show great sadness. Mourners also sometimes sprinkled ashes on their heads or sat in a pile of ashes to show how sorrowful they felt (Valetta et al., *Families,* 7).

King Hezekiah and the Prophet Isaiah

The Healing of Hezekiah

King Hezekiah became very ill. At first, Isaiah told Hezekiah that he was going to die, but Hezekiah prayed that he would be able to live longer. As Isaiah was leaving, he heard the voice of the Lord telling him to go back to Hezekiah. Isaiah returned and blessed Hezekiah to be healed. Hezekiah lived for fifteen more years.

The Writings of Isaiah

Seven hundred years before Jesus Christ was born, Isaiah wrote about the Savior's birth and life and about His second coming in the latter days. Jesus himself quoted from Isaiah's writings more than from those of any other prophet. The Book of Mormon includes whole passages from Isaiah. The Lord taught the Nephites that "great are the words of Isaiah" (3 Nephi 23:1).

King Hezekiah ruled over Judah, the southern kingdom of Israel, for almost thirty years. He trusted God and kept His commandments, and he took counsel from the prophet Isaiah.

Hezekiah was twenty-five years old when he became king. One of the first things he did was destroy the idols and the high places and groves where his people had been worshipping false gods. He even broke the brazen serpent that Moses had created in the wilderness, because the people were worshipping it like an idol. He wanted his people to turn to the one true God who had led and guided their ancestors.

Fourteen years after Hezekiah became king of Judah, King Sennacherib of Assyria attacked his kingdom. Hezekiah sent messengers to the Assyrian king, offering to pay whatever he asked if he would take his army and leave their land in peace. Sennacherib said he wanted three hundred talents of silver and thirty talents of gold. Hezekiah gave him all of the silver from the temple and the gold stripped from the temple doors. Sennacherib took all of the gold and silver, but then he demanded the surrender of Jerusalem anyway.

Hezekiah did not know what to do. He went to the temple and prayed that the Lord would save his people from the Assyrians. He sent for the prophet Isaiah. Isaiah told Hezekiah's servants to tell the king not to be afraid because the Lord would protect them. Isaiah promised that not even an arrow would fly against Jerusalem and that the king of Assyria would go back the way he had come.

The Assyrian army closed in on Jerusalem. That very night, the Lord sent an angel to the Assyrian camp, and by morning, 185,000 soldiers lay dead. When Sennacherib awoke and saw how his army had perished, he turned back to his own country. Jerusalem was safe in the care of King Hezekiah, a ruler who trusted God more than he feared men.

King Josiah

Scroll of the Law

In ancient times, the scriptures were handwritten on parchment, or animal skin, and rolled into scrolls. The scrolls were kept by the priests. The people did not have their own copies of the scriptures.

Rending the Clothes

Anciently, people would rend, or tear, their clothes to show their deep sorrow or distress.

After his father had been killed by his own servants, eight-year-old prince Josiah became king of Judah. Josiah's father and grandfather had been wicked men, but Josiah wanted to keep the commandments and please the Lord.

After he had been king for eighteen years, Josiah wanted to repair the temple. He hired carpenters, builders, and masons. He arranged to have stone cut and timber carried to the site to restore the house of the Lord. While they were working in the temple, the high priest Hilkiah found the book of the law, or the scriptures. It had been lost for a long time. Hilkiah gave the book to the scribe, and the scribe read it to King Josiah.

When Josiah heard the scribe read the law, he realized how wicked the people of his kingdom had become. He rent, or tore, his clothes to show how worried and troubled he was that his people had forgotten the commandments and turned away from the true and living God. He asked his advisers to find the prophetess Huldah and seek her counsel. Huldah told King Josiah that, indeed, the kingdom of Judah had lost favor with the Lord, but because the king was so humble and his heart was so tender, the Lord would be merciful to him.

King Josiah summoned his people to gather at the temple. He explained how the scriptures had been found, and he read to them all the words of the book of the law. Before all the people, King Josiah promised to keep the Lord's commandments and to follow Him. The people joined their king and covenanted to obey God's word.

King Josiah removed all of the idols from the temple and destroyed the high places and groves where the people worshipped false gods. He burned the idols and images and tore down the buildings where evil practices were performed. King Josiah commanded the people to join him in keeping the Passover, the ancient feast that celebrated the Israelites' deliverance from destruction and slavery.

King Josiah devoted his life to serving the Lord. No king before him had turned to the Lord with all his heart and soul as King Josiah did.

The Prophet Jeremiah

Lehi

The Book of Mormon prophet Lehi lived in Jerusalem at the same time as Jeremiah. Lehi was commanded to take his family and leave Jerusalem, but Jeremiah was told to stay and warn the people of their eventual destruction if they did not repent.

Baruch

Baruch, a friend of Jeremiah, was a scribe who wrote Jeremiah's prophecies on a scroll and read them to the people.

Even before Jeremiah was born, the Lord called him to be a prophet. When he was a young man, Jeremiah was afraid that he would not be able to speak well as the Lord's messenger. But the Lord told him not to be afraid. He touched Jeremiah's mouth and promised He would give Jeremiah the words he should speak.

Jeremiah served as a prophet during the reign of the last three kings of Judah: Josiah, Jehoiakim, and Zedekiah. King Josiah was a righteous king who listened to the prophets and obeyed the word of God, but the kings who came after him did not like hearing what the prophets said. Jeremiah prophesied that Jerusalem would be destroyed if the kings and the people did not repent.

The people became angry with Jeremiah, and they wanted to silence him. The Lord told Jeremiah to stand at the city gate and proclaim that trouble would come if the people continued their wickedness. The overseer of the temple stopped Jeremiah, beat him, and held him in the stocks. Another time, Jeremiah was thrown into a muddy dungeon for many days.

The Lord told Jeremiah to visit a potter's shop. As Jeremiah watched the potter work, he noticed how the potter shaped the clay and carefully smoothed the rough spots. Jeremiah told the people that the Lord wanted them to be like clay in the potter's hand. They needed to trust God and allow Him to shape their lives. But the people were too hard-hearted to listen.

Even King Zedekiah refused to listen to Jeremiah's counsel. To keep Jerusalem from being burned, the prophet encouraged the king to surrender to Babylon. Jeremiah prophesied that King Zedekiah would be delivered into the hands of the king of Babylon and taken away to that strange land. King Zedekiah did not want to hear any more of Jeremiah's prophecies, and he put Jeremiah in prison.

Just as the prophet had predicted, Jerusalem fell captive to Babylon, and Zedekiah became subject to Babylon's king, Nebuchadnezzar. Some of the people escaped to Egypt, taking Jeremiah with them. He died in Egypt, filled with sorrow and grief about what had happened to the kingdom of Judah.

Stocks

Used as a punishment, stocks were wooden frames with holes to hold the hands and feet. When a prisoner was locked into the stocks, he or she was not able to move.

Lamentations

Jeremiah wrote many poems of mourning and grief that showed his sadness about the captivity of his people. We can read these poems, called lamentations, in the book of Lamentations in the Bible.

The Prophet Daniel

Pulse

Pulse is made up of seeds and grains, such as peas, beans, lentils, wheat, barley, or rye (OT student manual 2:298).

The Lost Tribes of Israel

After two hundred years of apostasy and nineteen kings, the kingdom of Israel was captured by Assyria and its people were carried away. Because they were dispersed among the nations, these people are known as the "lost tribes" of Israel. Their "gathering" again in the last days has been prophesied since the days of their captivity. The kingdom of Judah was also captured, by Babylon, but after many years they were allowed to return to their homeland.

King Nebuchadnezzar stole precious vessels from the temple, but even worse, he took to Babylon many Jewish children who were smart, handsome, and skillful. Daniel and three of his friends lived in the king's palace, learned his language, and received training in the ways of the Babylonians.

When the king's servant offered Daniel rich meat to eat and wine to drink, Daniel told him that God had said not to eat and drink those things. Daniel convinced the servant to bring Daniel and his friends pulse to eat and water to drink. After ten days, they looked more healthy and handsome than ever. As they grew, the Lord blessed them with more wisdom and skill than the king's magicians and astrologers had.

Nebuchadnezzar was troubled by a dream, and none of his magicians and astrologers could tell him the dream or what it meant. He was angry, and he threatened to kill all of the wise men in Babylon—including Daniel and his friends. Daniel and his friends prayed for help. Daniel had a vision of the king's dream. He saw a great statue and a stone that was cut, without hands, out of the mountain. The stone struck the statue, breaking it in pieces, and then grew into a great mountain that filled the whole earth. Daniel told the king that the Lord had helped him understand that the statue represented Babylon and other earthly kingdoms. The stone represented the kingdom of God, the greatest kingdom of all. Nebuchadnezzar fell down and praised Daniel's God. He made Daniel a leader in the land.

Belshazzar, the new king of Babylon, hosted a great feast. The people drank wine from the sacred vessels from the temple in Jerusalem. Suddenly, a man's finger appeared and wrote words on the wall. The king was so afraid that his knees knocked together. None of his wise men could understand the writing on the wall. The queen remembered Daniel and his spiritual gifts. Daniel said the words meant that the king's reign was over, and his kingdom would soon be divided. That very night, the Medes and Persians slew Belshazzar and conquered Babylon, as Daniel had foretold.

The new king, Darius, made Daniel president over the princes of his kingdom. The princes were jealous of Daniel and wanted to find a way to make the king unhappy with him, but they could find no fault in him. The princes decided to convince the king to create a law that they knew Daniel would break. Not realizing they were trying to trap Daniel, the king signed a decree that for the next thirty days no one should ask a favor of any god or any man except the king. If anyone were caught praying to any god, he or she would be thrown into a den of lions.

Regardless of the new law, Daniel knelt down three times a day, giving thanks and praise to God. He did not close the windows or try to hide. As they had planned, the princes caught Daniel and brought him before the king. When Darius realized what had happened, he tried to change the law and save Daniel, but it was too late. Daniel was thrown into the lions' den.

The king fasted all night for Daniel's safety. He could not sleep. Early the next morning, he ran to the lions' den and called to Daniel—and Daniel answered. God had sent an angel to shut the lions' mouths, and Daniel was unharmed. The king rejoiced that Daniel had been spared because of his faith in God. Darius proclaimed throughout the land that Daniel's God was the true and living God.

Daniel's Accusers

The king commanded that Daniel's accusers be thrown into the lions' den. The lions broke their bones into pieces before their bodies reached the bottom of the den (Daniel 6:24).

Eighty Years Old

Many years passed between the time Daniel was taken to Nebuchadnezzar's court and the reign of King Darius. Daniel was probably about eighty years old when he was thrown into the den of lions (Rasmussen, *Commentary*, 621).

Shadrach, Meshach, and Abed-nego

New Names

In Babylon, Daniel and his friends were given new names. Daniel was called *Belteshazzar,* Hananiah became *Shadrach,* Mishael became *Meshach,* and Azariah became *Abed-nego.*

Musical Instruments

Ancient musical instruments mentioned in Daniel 3 include the *cornet,* a brass instrument similar to a trumpet; the *sackbut,* a triangle-shaped instrument with strings; and the *psaltery,* a stringed instrument similar to a small harp. The *flute* and *harp* that are mentioned were probably similar in many ways to the flute and harp of today.

Cornet

Nebuchadnezzar, the king of Babylon, built a golden statue more than a hundred feet tall. He gathered the princes, governors, captains, and rulers for its dedication. The king ordered a messenger to announce to all the people that whenever they heard the music of the cornet, flute, harp, sackbut, psaltery, and dulcimer, they must bow down and worship the statue. Nebuchadnezzar warned the people that if they refused to bow to the statue, they would be thrown into a fiery furnace.

The king's advisers reported that certain Jews whom the king had made rulers in Babylon would not worship the golden statue. The Jews' names were Shadrach, Meshach, and Abed-nego, and they did not bow down when the music sounded. Nebuchadnezzar ordered Shadrach, Meshach, and Abed-nego to be brought before him. He asked them if what he had heard about them were true, and he gave them one more chance to bow to the golden statue. He threatened to throw them into a fiery furnace if they refused—and he boldly declared that their God would not be able to save them.

Shadrach, Meshach, and Abed-nego loved God more than they feared the king or his fiery furnace. They told the king that they would worship only the true and living God—even if it meant their death. Nebuchadnezzar immediately commanded that the furnace be heated seven times hotter than its usual temperature. His servants bound Shadrach, Meshach, and Abed-nego and threw them into the furnace.

The fire burned with such intensity that the servants themselves perished—but Shadrach, Meshach, and Abed-nego did not. Suddenly, King Nebuchadnezzar asked his servants why he saw four men walking, unhurt, in the fire when only three were thrown in. The king said the fourth person looked like the Son of God. He called to Shadrach, Meshach, and Abed-nego to come out of the furnace.

The princes, governors, and other officers gathered around to see what had happened. The three faithful Jews were completely unharmed. The fire had not ignited their clothes or singed their hair, and they didn't even smell like smoke.

King Nebuchadnezzar praised the God of Shadrach, Meshach, and Abed-nego, who had sent an angel to deliver his servants because they trusted in him.

Psaltery and flutes

Harp

Queen Esther

A Jewish man named Mordecai lived in Shushan, the capital of Persia. Mordecai had a younger cousin named Esther. When Esther's parents died, Mordecai took her into his home and raised her as his own daughter. She grew to be a beautiful young woman.

The Persian emperor Ahasuerus commanded his servants to find him a new queen. The servants gathered Esther and many other young women from the kingdom to the palace to meet the king. Mordecai went to the palace every day to watch over Esther and see what would become of her. Mordecai had told Esther not to reveal that she was a Jew because many Persians were not friendly to the Jewish people.

All of the young women were brought before the king, but when he met Esther, he loved her more than all the others. He placed the royal crown upon her head and made her the queen of Persia. The king held a great wedding feast and invited all of the princes and servants to come. Mordecai was made a keeper of the king's gate.

King Ahasuerus appointed a man named Haman to be his chief minister over the princes and servants and commanded that everyone bow to him. But whenever Haman walked through the palace gates, Mordecai would not bow to him like the others. Mordecai's refusal to bow before anyone but God made Haman very angry.

The King's Ring

Kings wore rings with a stamp, called a seal, engraved on them. The king dipped the ring in wax and put his stamp of authority on official documents. The people knew that they must obey what was written in the documents.

When Haman learned that Mordecai was a Jew, he wanted to get rid of all of the Jews in the kingdom. Haman told the king that there were certain people in his kingdom who did not keep the king's laws, and they should be destroyed. The king trusted Haman, so he gave him his ring with his seal on it and told Haman to do what seemed best to him. Haman wrote an order that on a certain day all the Jews in the kingdom were to be destroyed, and he sealed it with the king's ring.

When Mordecai heard the king's decree, he tore his clothes, put on sackcloth and ashes, and stood at the king's gate, weeping and mourning. He sent a servant to his cousin Esther, asking her to go before the king and plead for her people. At first, Esther was afraid. She knew that if someone went into the king's court without being invited, that person might be put to death unless the king held out his scepter toward him or her. Mordecai reminded Esther that if Haman's decree were carried out, she would be killed, too, because she was a Jew. He gently suggested that perhaps God had helped her become queen so that she could save her people.

Esther instructed the servant to tell Mordecai to ask all the Jewish people to join with her and her servants in fasting for three days, and then she would go to the king and ask for his help. Esther trusted God and was willing to risk her life to save her people.

Three days later, Esther put on her royal clothing and stood in the inner court of the king's house as the king sat upon his throne. When the king saw Esther, he held out his golden scepter to her. She walked to the throne and touched the top of the scepter. Esther invited the king and Haman to join her at a banquet that she had prepared for them. At the banquet, Esther explained to the king who she was and that her people were going to be destroyed because of Haman's decree. The king became angry and ordered that Haman be hanged. The king took the ring he had given to Haman and gave it to Mordecai instead. Letters were sent throughout the kingdom, putting an end to Haman's decree. Esther and her people were saved.

The King's Scepter

A scepter was a staff carried by kings to show their authority (Valetta et al., *Families,* 398).

Job

Yoke

A yoke is a wooden bar or collar that is placed over the necks of two animals, such as oxen, to enable them to walk and work together.

Boils

Boils are infected sores on the skin that are painful and may cause a fever.

Perhaps a thousand years before Jesus was born, a man named Job lived in the land of Uz. Job was a very righteous man who loved God and offered sacrifices to Him. The Lord blessed Job and his wife abundantly. They had a large family of seven sons and three daughters. Job was also blessed to own a great deal of property. He had seven thousand sheep, three thousand camels, five hundred yoke of oxen, and five hundred female donkeys.

Satan told the Lord that he believed Job trusted God only because Job had such a good life. The Lord assured Satan that Job would remain faithful no matter what happened to him.

One day a messenger came to Job with bad news. While Job's servants were plowing his fields and feeding his donkeys, some strangers had attacked them, killing the servants and taking the oxen and donkeys. The messenger had not finished speaking when another messenger came with more bad news. He reported that fire from heaven had struck Job's sheep and his servants in the field, killing them all. Almost immediately, a third messenger came. He said that three bands of outlaws had killed the servants who were guarding Job's camels and had stolen the camels. Then a final messenger came with the worst news of all. While Job's sons and daughters were feasting in the oldest son's house, a great wind had blown in from the wilderness, and the son's house had collapsed on all of Job's children, killing every one of them.

Job fell upon the ground and prayed to God. Even in his grief, Job remained faithful. He said that the Lord had given him everything he had, and now the Lord had taken it away. He did not turn away from God but praised Him and blessed His name.

Sometime later, Job was stricken with boils all over his body. From head to foot, Job was covered with painful sores. His wife began to lose faith. She wondered why Job still believed that God was good. But Job said that we need to be humble and trust God.

Job's friends came to visit him. Some of the things they said were comforting to him. But when they told him that God must be punishing him for being wicked, he knew they didn't understand. He had always tried to follow God's commandments, and now it seemed that God was not hearing his prayers. But even when he felt completely alone, Job expressed his faith in God. He said he knew that even if he were to die, someday he would be resurrected, and he would see God.

Finally, the Lord spoke to Job and showed Job His power. Job was humble and said he knew that God is great and that man doesn't know everything that God knows.

After much suffering, Job was healed. Because of his faith, the Lord blessed him with seven more sons and three beautiful daughters and twice as much property as he had before. Job lived to see four generations of his family and died at a very old age.

Zacharias, Elisabeth, and John

Naming Children

Eight days after a baby boy was born, Jewish parents held a special ceremony and gave the child a name.

More than two thousand years ago, a priest named Zacharias and his wife, Elisabeth, lived near Jerusalem. They were good people who obeyed God's commandments. They had prayed for a child for many years, but they had become old and had never had children.

One day while Zacharias was serving in the temple, he was alone by the altar of incense. Suddenly, an angel of the Lord appeared to him. At first, Zacharias felt afraid, but the angel said, "Fear not, for thy prayer is heard." The angel introduced himself as Gabriel. He told Zacharias that his wife would give birth to a son, who should be named John. The angel told Zacharias that he and Elisabeth would have joy and gladness in their son because he would be great in the Lord's sight. Even before his birth, their baby would be filled with the Holy Ghost.

Zacharias questioned how all of this could be possible since he and his wife were too old to have children. Gabriel told Zacharias that because he

Writing Table (or Tablet)

Before paper was readily available, a writing table, or tablet, was used. The tablet was usually a small wooden board covered with a layer of wax. Writing was done by pressing letters into the wax with a pointed instrument (Ogden and Skinner, *Gospels,* 47).

had not believed the angel's words, he would be struck dumb and would not be able to speak until after the baby was born. When Zacharias walked out of the temple, the people wondered why he had been there so long. And when he could not speak to them, they knew that he had seen a vision. Zacharias returned to his home in the hill country near Jerusalem. A little while later, just as the angel foretold, Elisabeth was expecting a baby.

The angel Gabriel also visited Elisabeth's younger cousin Mary. He gave Mary some wonderful news of her own: she was to become the mother of the Son of God. The angel then told Mary that her cousin Elisabeth, whom many thought was too old to have a child, was going to have a baby. The angel reminded Mary that "with God nothing shall be impossible."

Mary quickly left her home and went to stay with Elisabeth. When Mary greeted her cousin, the baby inside Elisabeth leaped for joy! The Holy Ghost filled Elisabeth's heart, and she knew Mary was blessed above all women. Mary would give birth to the Son of God. Mary stayed with Elisabeth for three months.

As foretold, Elisabeth gave birth to a son. Their family and friends thought Zacharias and Elisabeth would name the boy after his father, but Elisabeth said his name would be John. When they questioned Zacharias about the name, he asked for a writing table and wrote, "His name is John." Immediately, Zacharias could speak again. He praised God and prophesied that John would prepare the way for the Lord.

The Birth of Jesus Christ

Swaddling Clothes

Swaddling clothes are strips of linen cloth that mothers wrap tightly around their newborns to help them feel secure and warm.

Mary was a most righteous and beautiful young woman who lived in Nazareth. Mary loved Joseph, a carpenter who was a good man, and Joseph loved Mary. They were going to be married.

One day an angel named Gabriel appeared to Mary. He told her that she was going to have a baby and that she should name him Jesus. Mary did not understand how she, a young, unmarried woman, would have a baby. The angel explained to her that Heavenly Father would be the baby's father. Mary would be the mother of the Son of God.

When Joseph heard that Mary was going to have a baby, he wondered what to do. In those days, if a Jewish woman had a baby before she was married, she could be put on trial and even killed. Joseph loved Mary and wanted to protect her. He thought he should end their engagement privately, so she would not have to go to trial. But Joseph had a dream in which an angel told him that Mary's baby would save the people from their sins. The angel told him that he should not hesitate to make Mary his wife and that when the baby was born, his name should be Jesus.

Mary and Joseph were married. About the time when the baby was to be born, they traveled eighty miles to Bethlehem, their ancestors' hometown, to pay taxes. By the time they arrived in Bethlehem, after several days' journey, all the inns were full. But Mary and Joseph found a place to stay. The baby Jesus was born in a stable. Mary wrapped him in swaddling clothes and laid him in a manger.

Not far away, shepherds were watching over their flocks during the night. An angel appeared and told them that the Savior was born! The glory of the Lord lit up the night sky, and a whole host of angels sang praises to God.

The shepherds ran to see the newborn King. Just as the angel had told them, the shepherds found Mary and Joseph, with the baby Jesus wrapped in swaddling clothes and lying in a manger. The shepherds told everyone what they had seen and heard. They glorified and praised God because the Savior of the world had been born.

Manger

A manger is a feeding trough for animals. In the ancient world, it was usually made of stone (Proctor and Proctor, *Source,* 49).

Jesus as a Child

Requirements of the Law of Moses

The law of Moses prohibited Jewish mothers from going out in public for forty days after a male child was born or eighty days after a female child was born. After this amount of time had passed, parents were required by the law to bring an offering to the temple. If they had enough money, they brought a lamb and a pigeon or a turtledove. But if, like Mary and Joseph, they had little money, they brought two pigeons or two turtledoves (McConkie, *DNTC* 1:99).

Prophetess

A prophetess is a woman who receives revelation from the Holy Ghost that Jesus is the Christ (Revelation 19:10; McConkie, *DNTC* 1:101).

Forty days after Jesus was born, Joseph and Mary brought him to the temple to present him to the Lord. Obeying the law of Moses, they also brought an offering of two turtledoves or pigeons.

An elderly man named Simeon saw the baby Jesus in the temple that day. He asked Joseph and Mary if he could hold their baby. Simeon was a righteous man who came to the temple often. The Holy Ghost had made it known to Simeon that he would see the Savior before he died, and the Holy Ghost had prompted Simeon to come to the temple that very day. When Simeon saw Jesus, the Holy Ghost revealed to him that this baby was Christ the Lord. He took the baby in his arms and blessed God. He prayed that he could die in peace now that he had seen the Christ. Simeon prophesied that this baby would be a light to others and that he would be the Savior of the world. Joseph and Mary marveled at all that Simeon said, and Simeon blessed them.

Just then an elderly woman named Anna approached Joseph and Mary in the temple. She, too, bore witness that the baby would be the Savior of the world. Anna was more than a hundred years old. She fasted and

Gold, Frankincense, and Myrrh

Gold is a precious metal. Frankincense is a resin, or a kind of sap, that comes from certain trees; when the dried and hardened frankincense is burned, it has a pleasant odor. Myrrh is a blend of oil and resin; it may be used as a medicine or perfume, or it may be burned like frankincense for its pleasant odor.

John the Baptist

John was six months older than Jesus. When Herod ordered the male children to be killed, Zacharias told Elisabeth to take John to the mountains, where he would be safe (Smith, *Teachings*, 261).

prayed often and served in the temple every day. Anna was a prophetess. She knew the baby who had been brought to the temple that day was the Son of God, and she thanked God for sending the Redeemer to the world.

After Jesus was born in Bethlehem, a bright new star in the sky led some wise men from the East to the land where Jesus lived. The wise men asked Herod, the king of Judea, where to find the child who was born to be King of the Jews. Herod was troubled by their questions. He demanded that his chief priests and scribes tell him where the new king would be born. They said the prophets had written that he would be born in Bethlehem.

Herod asked the wise men to bring him word when they had found the child. Herod told them he wanted to worship the newborn king, but in reality he wanted to destroy him.

At last, the wise men found the young child, Jesus, in his home with his mother, Mary. When they saw Jesus, the wise men bowed before him and worshipped him. They gave him gifts of gold, frankincense, and myrrh. The wise men were warned in a dream that they should not return to Herod. Instead, they returned to their own country by a different road.

When Herod learned that the wise men had left the country without telling him where to find Jesus, he was furious. He sent his soldiers from house to house in Bethlehem and the surrounding area, ordering them to kill every male child under the age of two.

An angel warned Joseph in a dream that Herod would seek the child to destroy him. During the night, Joseph took Mary and Jesus and escaped to Egypt as the angel had instructed. They lived there until Herod died and an angel told them it was safe to go home. In Nazareth, Jesus learned and grew and found favor with God and man.

The Boy Jesus in the Temple

Unleavened Bread

One of the traditional foods of the Passover feast is unleavened bread. It is made without yeast, so it remains flat and does not rise. When the ancient Israelites were freed from slavery and left Egypt, they were in such a hurry that they did not have time to let their bread rise. The leavening, or yeast, in bread is also a symbol of pride or sin that "puffs" people up and leads them away from God (Bible Dictionary, 723). Eating unleavened bread helped the Jews remember to be humble and remember God's goodness.

Every spring, Jewish families traveled to the temple in Jerusalem. There they made sacred offerings and celebrated the Feast of the Passover, a special time for Jews to remember how the Lord delivered their ancestors from slavery in Egypt. When a Jewish family arrived in the city, they went to the temple to make a sacred offering of a lamb or a goat. They ate a dinner that included special foods, such as unleavened bread, to remember that the Lord had blessed them and their ancestors with freedom. The celebration usually lasted for a week, and then the families returned to their homes.

When Jesus was twelve years old, he and his family lived in Nazareth. They traveled several days to Jerusalem for the feast. At the end of Passover week, Jesus' family left Jerusalem to return to Nazareth. Mary and Joseph traveled a whole day before they realized that Jesus was not with them. They hurried back to Jerusalem. After looking for Jesus for three days, they found him in the temple. He was talking with the doctors and other men of learning. They were hearing him and asking him questions. They were all amazed at the things Jesus knew and understood.

Worried and tired, Mary told Jesus that they had been looking for him for several days. She and Joseph wondered if he had been hurt or lost. But Jesus wondered why they were looking for him. He thought they would know that he needed to be doing his Heavenly Father's business—teaching in the temple.

Jesus left Jerusalem with Mary and Joseph and returned to their home in Nazareth. Mary pondered what Jesus had been doing in the temple. She knew he was God's son and that his life would be spent in God's service.

Carpentry

Joseph was a carpenter, or woodworker, and he most likely taught Jesus woodworking skills. They probably made tools, furniture, and other household items.

Jesus Begins His Ministry

Locusts

Locusts are a kind of grasshopper that is plentiful in desert regions. Some locusts can be as long as six inches, and most are edible.

The Jordan River

The Jordan River flows out of the Sea of Galilee and into the Dead Sea. It is more than a hundred miles long and ranges in depth from three to twelve feet (Bible Dictionary, 716). Hundreds of years before Jesus was baptized in the Jordan River, the Israelites crossed this river on their way to Jericho in the promised land.

Zacharias and Elisabeth's son, John, whose birth was a miracle, became a prophet who prepared the people to receive Jesus Christ. John preached in the wilderness. He wore clothes made of camel's hair and leather, and he ate locusts and wild honey. He kept the commandments of God and taught the people to repent.

Some religious leaders of the day taught that anyone who came from the family of Abraham would be saved. John taught that all people must have faith, repent, and be baptized in order to be saved. Most important, John was called to prepare the people to receive the Savior. John explained that he did not feel worthy to even loosen the straps of Jesus' shoes for him as a servant would. When Jesus came from Galilee to the Jordan River to be baptized, John said he felt unworthy to baptize Jesus. Why would Jesus, who had never committed any sin, need to be baptized? Jesus explained that he needed to be baptized "to fulfill all righteousness." He knew that everyone needs to keep God's law of baptism, and he wanted to set an example for everyone to follow.

John baptized Jesus by lowering him under the water and raising him back up again. When Jesus came up out of the Jordan River, the heavens opened, and the Spirit of God came upon him. A dove appeared as a sign from Heavenly Father that the Holy Ghost was present. The people who were gathered at the river heard the voice of Heavenly Father speaking from heaven. He said, "This is my beloved Son, in whom I am well pleased." All three members of the Godhead—Heavenly Father, Jesus Christ, and the Holy Ghost—were present at Jesus' baptism.

Shortly after Jesus was baptized, the Spirit of the Lord led him into the wilderness to be with God. In the wilderness, Jesus fasted and prayed for forty days and forty nights. After forty days, Jesus was very hungry, and Satan tried to tempt him. Satan challenged Jesus: "If thou be the Son of God, command this stone that it be made bread." Jesus refused. He answered Satan with a scripture: "Man shall not live by bread alone, but by every word that proceedeth out of the mouth of God."

The Spirit of the Lord led Jesus to Jerusalem to the pinnacle of the temple. Again, Satan tried to tempt him. This time, he dared Jesus to leap off the temple to see if angels would catch him. Once more, Jesus

Jesus Knew the Scriptures

Each time Satan tried to tempt him, Jesus resisted him with a scripture. Compare these scriptures from the Old Testament—the scriptures Jesus would have learned as a child—with what Jesus said to Satan.

Deuteronomy 8:3: "Man doth not live by bread only, but by every word that proceedeth out of the mouth of the Lord doth man live."

Deuteronomy 6:16: "Ye shall not tempt the Lord your God."

Exodus 20:3: "Thou shalt have no other gods before me."

responded with a scripture: "It is written again, Thou shalt not tempt the Lord thy God."

Finally, the Spirit of the Lord led Jesus to an exceedingly high mountain where he was shown the kingdoms and the glory of the world. Trying to tempt Jesus a third time, Satan offered to give Jesus all the kingdoms and glory of the world if Jesus would bow down and worship him. This time Jesus commanded Satan to leave. He said, "Get thee hence, Satan." And again, he quoted a scripture: "Thou shalt worship the Lord thy God, and him only shalt thou serve."

Even though Jesus could have turned the stone into bread or ordered angels to catch him when he fell, and even though he already had power over all the kingdoms of the earth, he never used his power to serve himself, but only to serve others.

Pinnacle of the Temple

This may have been the highest corner of the wall around the Temple Mount in Jerusalem (Proctor and Proctor, *Source,* 63; Ogden and Skinner, *Gospels,* 94).

Miracle at the Marriage Feast

Wine

The wine served at the wedding feast was pure, fresh grape juice from the vine, the common drink of the time (Talmage, *Jesus the Christ,* 144).

Governor of the Feast

Usually a relative of the host or hostess, the governor of the feast was like the master of ceremonies who was in charge of what happened there.

After Jesus was baptized, disciples began to follow him, some of whom would become special witnesses of him. John the Baptist's testimony of Jesus so impressed Andrew and his friend John that they followed Jesus from that day on. When Andrew brought his brother Simon Peter to Jesus, Jesus called him Cephas, which means "a stone." Cephas, or Simon Peter, became a disciple of Jesus Christ.

On his way to Galilee, Jesus invited a man named Philip to follow him—and he did. Philip found his friend Nathanael and invited him to join them. When Jesus met Nathanael, he already knew about him. He told Nathanael that he knew he had been sitting under a fig tree before coming to meet Jesus. Nathanael was amazed at what Jesus knew. He, too, became his loyal disciple.

Jesus went with his disciples to a marriage feast in Galilee. Jesus' mother, Mary, was helping with the feast. She became concerned when there was no more wine for the guests to drink. Mary told Jesus about the problem, and Jesus offered to do what he could for her. He did not think the time had come for him to perform miracles in public, but he was willing to do whatever Mary needed him to do. She told the servants to follow Jesus' instructions.

Jesus told the servants to fill six stone pots with water. After the pots were filled to the brim, Jesus told the servants to serve the guests, starting with the governor of the feast. When the servants poured the water, it had changed to wine!

When the governor of the feast tasted the wine, he asked the bridegroom why he had saved the best wine for the end of the feast. Usually, people served the best wine first. The governor and the other guests did not know that Jesus had miraculously supplied the wine. This was the first of Jesus' many miracles that were recorded.

Jesus Cleanses the Temple

Every year, the Jewish people traveled to Jerusalem for the Feast of the Passover. During the feast, they remembered the way their Israelite ancestors had been freed from Egyptian slavery and destruction, and they made sacrificial offerings of oxen, sheep, and doves. The sacrifices showed their devotion to God and prepared them to understand the sacrifice that would someday be made by their Messiah, or Deliverer.

Jesus, too, traveled to the city for the celebration. When he approached the temple, he saw people selling oxen, sheep, and doves inside the temple courtyard. Jesus was unhappy that they had turned the holy temple into a noisy marketplace. He made a scourge, or small whip, of cords to drive the moneychangers and their animals out of the temple grounds. He waved his whip, overturned the tables, and told the people to take their animals and cages of doves and go. He rebuked them, telling them the temple was not a place for buying and selling things.

As Jesus drove the moneychangers out of the temple, his disciples, or followers, remembered a scripture that is now recorded in Psalm 69:9: "The zeal of thine house hath eaten me up," meaning "My devotion for the Lord's house consumes me." They saw how important it was to Jesus to make his Father's house clean and holy once again. He was doing what Heavenly Father wanted him to do.

Moneychangers

Ordinary money could not be used in the temple courtyard. Those coins were engraved with pictures of foreign kings or foreign gods, so the Jewish leaders did not want their people to buy sacred temple sacrifices with them. They ruled that the people could exchange Roman or other foreign coins for special temple coins. The moneychangers thrived because everyone had to use their services, and they often cheated people. Instead of arguing with them, Jesus took action and showed them that what they were doing was wrong (Talmage, *Jesus the Christ,* 154; McConkie, *DNTC* 1:137–38).

Scourge

A small whip or lash, usually made of several long, thin pieces of leather that may or may not be braided together.

The Woman at the Well

Waterpot

A waterpot was essential to homes in biblical times. Women carried water from wells or rivers every day to use for cooking, bathing, and drinking (Proctor and Proctor, *Source,* 70).

Jesus and his disciples left Judea and began walking to Galilee. Most Jews took the longer route that went around an area called Samaria because the Jews and the Samaritans were not friendly with each other. But Jesus led his disciples on the shorter route that went directly through Samaria. While his disciples were buying food in a Samaritan town, Jesus waited for them by a well of water known as Jacob's Well.

In the middle of the day, a Samaritan woman came to the well to fill her waterpot. Jesus greeted her and asked her for a drink. Because he was a Jew and she was a Samaritan, the woman was surprised that Jesus would speak to her. He told her that if she asked *him* for a drink, he would give her "living water." The woman did not understand what Jesus meant. He explained that those who drink of the living water He offers will never be thirsty again but will have within themselves a well of water that will lead them to eternal life.

The woman asked him to give her some of that water so she would not have to walk to the well each day. She did not understand that Jesus was not talking about physical water but about his teachings and his Atonement that would enable God's children to return to live with Him someday.

Jesus asked the woman to call her husband to come. She responded that she did not have a husband. Jesus told her he was already aware that she had had five husbands in the past and that she now was not married.

The Samaritan woman said that she could see that Jesus was a prophet because, even though she had told him nothing about herself, he knew all about her. She said that she believed a Messiah called Christ would someday come and teach the people all the things God wanted them to know. Jesus said to her, "I—the one who is speaking to you now—am he." Just then, Jesus' disciples returned. They were surprised to find Jesus speaking to a Samaritan woman.

The woman quickly went into the city, leaving the well in such a hurry that she did not even think to take her waterpot with her. She told the men of the city that she had met someone who could tell her everything she had ever done. She asked them, "Is not this the Christ?" Many of the Samaritans went to meet Jesus, and he stayed in their city for two days. Some of them believed in him because of the woman's testimony, and many more believed when they heard Jesus' own words. They knew that he was the Christ, the Savior of the world.

Jacob's Well

This well was not only a good source of water but it also had special meaning to the Israelites. The well was located on land owned anciently by their ancestor, the patriarch Jacob, or Israel (Talmage, *Jesus the Christ,* 172).

The Twelve Apostles

The Original Twelve Apostles

The names of Jesus' twelve apostles were Simon Peter; Andrew; James; John; Philip; Bartholomew; Matthew; Thomas; James, the son of Alphaeus; Simon Zelotes; Judas, the brother of James; and Judas Iscariot (Luke 6:13–16).

A crowd gathered by the Sea of Galilee to listen to Jesus teach. So many people wanted to be near Jesus that he stepped into Peter's boat that was waiting near the shore. Jesus asked Peter to push the boat a little way from the land. Sitting in the boat, Jesus could teach the people, and they could see and hear him.

When Jesus had finished speaking, he asked Peter to launch the boat into deeper waters and let down his fishing nets. Peter answered that he and his brother Andrew had been fishing all night and had caught nothing—but he obeyed and let down his net into the sea. Almost immediately, Peter and Andrew caught so many fish that their net began to break! Peter called their fishing partners, James and John, to help them bring in the fish. The partners brought their boat, and together they loaded both boats so full of fish that they began to sink.

Peter and the others were astonished at the number of fish they had caught. Peter fell down at Jesus' knees and exclaimed that he did not feel

worthy to be near the Lord. Jesus told Peter, Andrew, James, and John not to be afraid. He invited them to become "fishers of men." They would teach people the truth and bring them into his church. Straight away, these men abandoned their fishing and their boats and followed Jesus.

In another place, Jesus walked past a man named Matthew, who was working as a tax collector. Jesus invited Matthew to follow him, and Matthew immediately stood and followed Jesus.

Jesus chose these men and seven others to be apostles, or special witnesses of Jesus Christ to the world. When Jesus had called all twelve, he took them to a mountain and ordained them apostles, giving them priesthood authority. He taught them his gospel and prepared them to preach throughout the world. Jesus sent them, two by two, to call people to repentance, to cast out devils, and to anoint the sick and heal them. Sending them on their missions without purse or scrip, Jesus told them to be unselfish and not to think of themselves or their own needs. He promised that if they would "lose" their lives in this way, they would "find" even better lives, full of great joy and peace.

Without Purse or Scrip

A "purse" was a bag for holding money, and "scrip" was a bag, usually made of leather, for carrying bread or other food (Bible Dictionary, 770). Serving a mission "without purse or scrip" meant going forward with faith, not taking food or money or other supplies. The missionary did not know where he would sleep or what he would eat but relied on God's goodness for all his needs.

Jesus in Nazareth

Messiah

The Messiah was the king or deliverer whose coming had been prophesied many years before. Many of the Jews were expecting a messiah to deliver them from the Romans, who had political power over them. They did not recognize Jesus as the true Messiah, their spiritual King and Deliverer (Bible Dictionary, 731).

Jesus performed many miracles in Galilee, and then he returned to his hometown of Nazareth. Just as he had done ever since he was young, he went to the synagogue on the Sabbath day. As a child, he would have listened to others read the scriptures, but now that he was old

enough to be a teacher, he stood up to read. The caretaker of the scriptures handed him the book of Isaiah, and when Jesus opened it, he read: "The Spirit of the Lord is upon me, because he hath anointed me to preach the gospel to the poor; he hath sent me to heal the broken-hearted, to preach deliverance to the captives, and recovering of sight to the blind, to set at liberty them that are bruised."

When he finished reading, Jesus closed the book, gave it back to the caretaker, and sat down. Everyone in the synagogue stared at him. Jesus said, "This day is this scripture fulfilled in your ears." He was telling the people that he was the prophet Isaiah had written about in this scripture, the One who would come to heal and save his people. Those in the synagogue who had known Jesus since he was a child could not believe it. They said, "Is not this Joseph's son?" They couldn't understand how someone who had grown up in their town could be the promised Messiah, the Savior of the world.

Jesus did not seem surprised by their response. He said, "No prophet is accepted in his own country," and he recounted two scripture stories from ancient times to show them what he meant. He reminded the people that God had called a widow who was not an Israelite to feed his prophet Elijah during the years of terrible famine. He also recounted how, of all the lepers in Israel, the one who had faith enough to be healed was not an Israelite—he was Naaman, a Syrian.

When the people realized Jesus was implying that they, too, lacked faith and humility, they became angry. They stood and pushed Jesus out of the synagogue. They led him to the top of the hill upon which their city was built. They wanted to throw him over the side of the cliff, but he miraculously escaped. They did not see Jesus pass through the middle of the crowd and leave his hometown.

Synagogue

A synagogue is a Jewish meetinghouse, similar to a church building, where the Jews gather for their religious meetings.

The Sabbath Day

Sabbath Day

The Jews observed the Sabbath, their weekly holy day, from sundown on Friday night until sundown on Saturday night. They spoke certain prayers, ate certain foods, and rested from their regular work. Some Jewish leaders added extra religious rules to the law and forgot the main purpose of the Sabbath day: to worship God and do good things.

Adding to the Law of Moses

Over time, the Jewish leaders added rules and restrictions to the law of Moses that went beyond the original law. For example, the leaders said it was unlawful to walk on the grass, tie certain knots, make a fire, or have a broken bone fixed on the Sabbath day (McConkie, *DNTC* 1:188, 206).

When Jesus was in Jerusalem on the Sabbath day, he stopped at the pool of Bethesda by the sheep market. People who were sick or crippled gathered by the edge of the pool and waited for its waters to bubble. The people believed that the bubbling was caused by an angel stirring the water at certain times. They believed that whoever entered the pool first after the waters bubbled would be healed.

Jesus talked with a man by the pool who had suffered with a physical problem for thirty-eight years. The man waited at the water's edge, hoping to be the first one to get in, but he could not move on his own, and someone else always stepped into the pool before him. When Jesus asked the man if he wanted to be healed, the man explained that he needed someone to lift him into the water. Jesus knew the man did not need to go into the water to be healed. He commanded the man to stand, pick up his bed, and walk. Even though he had been crippled for many years, the man stood, picked up his bed, and walked away.

The Jews who did not have faith to believe in such a miracle tried to find something wrong with what Jesus had done. They said it was against Jewish law for Jesus to heal on the Sabbath and for the man to pick up his bed on the Sabbath. They were so angry with Jesus for breaking their laws that they wanted to kill him.

On another occasion, Jesus walked through a field of corn with his disciples on the Sabbath day. His disciples were hungry, and they picked some corn to eat. The Jewish leaders called Pharisees told Jesus it was against the law to pick corn on the Sabbath. Jesus reminded them that King David and his men had once been given bread from the temple to eat when they were in need. He declared to them that the Son of God is Lord of the Sabbath.

Later that day, Jesus entered the Jewish synagogue to teach the people. He healed a man with a withered hand and explained to the people that it is right to do good on the Sabbath day.

Pharisees

Some of the Jewish religious leaders called themselves Pharisees. They were proud of how strictly they observed the law of Moses, and they separated themselves from others to be sure they didn't touch anyone or anything that was considered unclean.

Jesus Heals

Leprosy

Leprosy is a skin disease so terrible it was called a "living death." People who suffered with leprosy were required to stay away from other people, and if anyone approached them, they warned the person, shouting, "Unclean!" (Bible Dictionary, 723–24).

Palsy

Palsy is a disease that causes paralysis, or loss of movement, as well as un-controlled body movements.

Jesus had the power to heal people of their sicknesses and disabilities. One day, as he walked through a crowd, a woman who had been bleeding for twelve years reached out and touched the hem of his clothing. Jesus turned to look at her. He told the woman that because of her great faith, she would be healed, and immediately her bleeding stopped.

A nobleman from Capernaum asked Jesus to come home with him and heal his son, who was near death. Jesus simply told the man that his son would live, and the man believed him. On his way home, the man met his servants, who had come to tell him that his son had not died but was alive. The man asked them what time his son had begun to improve—and it was the same hour that Jesus had said the son would live.

On another occasion, a man with leprosy pled with Jesus to heal him. Jesus had compassion on the man. He touched him with his hand, and immediately the leprosy was gone. Jesus sent the man to the priest to be cleansed according to the law of Moses. Word of the miracle spread, and soon, crowds of people followed Jesus wherever he went.

One time, the crowd was so large that some people carrying a paralyzed man on a portable bed could not get near Jesus. At last, the man's friends carried him to the rooftop of the house where Jesus was and lowered him through the roof. When Jesus saw their great faith, he forgave the sick man of his sins and healed him. The man picked up his bed and walked, and the people praised God.

Another day, an officer in the Roman army, a centurion, asked Jesus to help his servant, who was tormented with palsy. Fearing he was not worthy to have Jesus in his home, the centurion said he knew that if Jesus simply spoke the words, his servant would be healed. In that same hour, the servant was healed. Jesus told his followers that he had not seen such great faith even among God's people, the Israelites.

Near the Sea of Galilee, Jesus met a man who was deaf and could not speak. Jesus put his fingers in the man's ears, and then he spat and touched the man's tongue. He looked up to heaven and said, "Be opened." Immediately, the man's ears were opened and he could hear, and his tongue was loosed and he could speak.

One Sabbath day, Jesus met a man who had been blind since birth. Jesus' disciples asked whether it was the man's sins or his parents' sins that had caused the man's blindness. Jesus explained that the man was blind not because of sin but so the people could be shown the works of God. Jesus spat on the ground and made clay. He spread some clay on the blind man's eyes and told him to go wash in the pool of Siloam. When the man washed the clay from his eyes, he could see! His neighbors asked if he were the same blind man who had been begging in the streets, and the man said, "I am he." They asked him how his sight had been restored, and he told them about Jesus.

The people took the man to the Pharisees, who argued about whether Jesus could have the power of God if he healed on the Sabbath. When they questioned the man, he answered, "One thing I know: I was blind, and now I see." The Pharisees did not want to hear the man's testimony about Jesus, and they threw him out of their synagogue.

When Jesus heard what the Pharisees had done, he found the man and talked with him. He asked the man if he believed in the Son of God. The man bowed before Jesus and worshipped him, saying, "I believe."

Pool of Siloam

In the days of King Hezekiah of Judah (about 700 B.C.), a tunnel was built to bring water from a natural spring outside Jerusalem's city walls to the man-made pool of Siloam inside the city. During the Feast of Tabernacles in Jesus' day, the priest carried water in a golden pitcher from the pool of Siloam to the temple (Talmage, *Jesus the Christ*, 402–3, 421).

Other Healings of the Blind

Jesus restored sight to many who were blind. On one occasion, two blind men called out to Jesus, asking him to heal them. He touched their eyes and blessed them to be healed according to their faith—and they received their sight (Matthew 9:27–29).

The Sermon on the Mount

Beatitudes

At the beginning of his sermon, Jesus talked about several things we need to do in order to be "blessed," such as being gentle, forgiving, and merciful, being pure in heart, and being peacemakers. His teachings in this sermon that begin with "Blessed are" have come to be known as the Beatitudes (Matthew 5:3–11; 3 Nephi 12).

Book of Mormon Sermon

Jesus gave a very similar sermon to the people in the Americas when He visited them after His resurrection. This sermon is found in the Book of Mormon (3 Nephi 12).

One day, Jesus sat on the side of a hill so that all of his listeners could see and hear him. He taught them truths they needed to know to be happy and to return to live with Heavenly Father. He told the people they would be blessed for doing what is right and for believing in him. He taught them to be kind to everyone, to freely share their possessions, and to keep their promises.

Some of Jesus' teachings were unlike anything the people had heard before. He taught them to love their enemies, to pray for people who were unkind to them, and to do good things even for those who treated them badly because of their beliefs.

Jesus taught the people to seek eternal treasures—things of lasting worth—not earthly treasures that can rust or be eaten by moths. The things we think about and care about most are the things we "treasure." If our hearts are full of love, wisdom, and other good qualities, we will be able to enjoy those "treasures" forever.

Jesus helped the people understand what it means to have faith and to depend on Heavenly Father. Birds do not plant the seeds they eat, but Heavenly Father makes sure they have food. Lilies in the field grow beautifully without worrying about how they look or how they will grow. We, too, can trust that Heavenly Father watches over us.

In his sermon, Jesus taught important things about prayer. He said that hypocrites, or people who pretend to be more righteous than they really are, pray on street corners or in the synagogue where others can see them. But Jesus encouraged people to shut their doors and pray to Heavenly

Father where only He can hear them. Jesus taught that when we pray, we should speak from our hearts, asking God for the things we need.

Jesus even gave an example of how to pray. He began by addressing his Heavenly Father: *"Our Father which art in heaven, Hallowed be thy name."*

To show that we must be humble and recognize that Heavenly Father gives us all that we have, he prayed, *"Thy kingdom come. Thy will be done in earth, as it is in heaven. Give us this day our daily bread."*

Jesus taught us to pray for forgiveness and to be forgiving when he said, *"And forgive us our debts, as we forgive our debtors."*

He showed us how to ask for spiritual strength when he pled with Heavenly Father, *"And lead us not into temptation, but deliver us from evil."*

He finished his prayer by praising God, saying, *"For thine is the kingdom, and the power, and the glory, forever. Amen."*

Jesus also taught the people about fasting. He said that hypocrites fast with sad looks on their faces so others will know they are going without food. But those who fast with the right feeling in their hearts look their best so that others do not even know they are fasting. When we fast and pray privately, our Heavenly Father rewards us openly.

Jesus finished his sermon on the mount by saying that those who truly listen to his teachings and keep the commandments are like a wise man who builds his house upon a rock. When the rains come and the winds blow, the house on the rock stands firm. But those who do not listen to Jesus and keep the commandments are like a foolish man who builds his house upon sand. When the rains come and the winds blow, the house on the sand washes away. In our lives, the gospel of Jesus Christ will help us endure the trials that come to us. Jesus is the "rock" upon which we must build our "house" of faith.

A Light to the World

When we light a candle, we do not hide its light under a basket. We put it on a candlestick so that we can use and enjoy the light. Jesus wants us to share the spiritual light of the gospel with others. We need to let the light of our testimony shine for the whole world to see (Luke 5:14–15).

Salt of the Earth

In Jesus' sermon, those who faithfully live the gospel are compared to salt. In the same way that salt preserves food and gives it flavor, those who live the gospel of Jesus Christ preserve righteousness on the earth. Their lives have purpose and meaning, and they help others to grow in righteousness and happiness (Matthew 5:13).

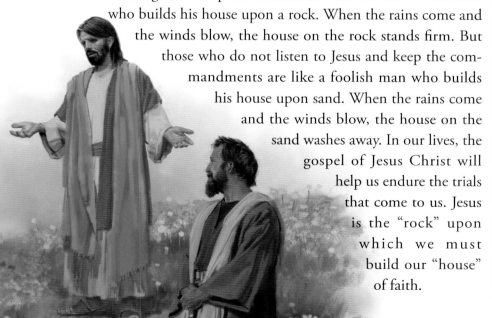

Jesus Forgives Sins

Pence

One pence was approximately the amount of money that a common laborer earned for one day of work (Brown et al., *Beholding Salvation,* 49).

Jesus not only healed people's bodies when they were sick or disabled but he also healed their spirits when they were sad about doing something wrong. He forgave their sins.

One woman felt very sorry for the mistakes she had made. When she heard that Jesus was eating at the home of a man named Simon, she went to see him there. The woman was weeping so much that she knelt down and washed Jesus' feet with her tears. She kissed his feet and wiped them with her hair to show how deeply she wanted to be forgiven of her sins. She had brought some precious cream, or ointment, and she rubbed it on Jesus' feet.

Simon was a Pharisee, or a member of a group of Jews who prided themselves in following religious laws with exactness. Simon wondered if Jesus knew he was letting a sinner touch him. But Jesus did know about her sins, and he also knew what the Pharisee was thinking. Jesus responded to Simon by telling him a story: Two people owed the same man some money. One person owed the man five hundred pence, and the other person owed him fifty pence. Neither one could pay the money he owed. The man decided to forgive them both, so they no longer needed to pay him. Jesus asked Simon which of the two men who had owed money loved the man most after he forgave them. Simon supposed the one who had owed the most money would be the one who loved the man most.

Jesus agreed with Simon. Then he pointed out that Simon, who thought he was very righteous, had not given Jesus water to wash his feet, greeted him with a kiss, or given him precious ointment. But this woman, who had committed many sins, had shown more love for Jesus by doing all of these things. She also

showed her faith in him by wanting to repent and be forgiven. Jesus turned to the woman and told her that her many sins were forgiven. He told her to leave in peace, that her faith had saved her.

On another occasion, Jesus went to the temple early in the morning to teach the people. The Pharisees brought to him a woman who had committed a very serious sin. According to their law, the punishment for such a sin was for the people to throw stones at her. The Pharisees wanted to see if Jesus would say that she should be stoned. If he didn't, they would accuse him of not showing respect for the law.

Jesus understood their evil purposes, and at first he did not answer them. He stooped down and wrote on the ground with his finger. When they insisted that he give them an answer, he finally invited them to think about their own lives. He said that if any of the Pharisees had never committed a sin, they should be the first ones to throw stones at the woman. The Pharisees knew they were not sinless, and one by one they left. When they had all gone, Jesus asked the woman where her accusers were. When she said that none of them remained, Jesus told her that he did not accuse her either. He told her to go and sin no more.

Seating at the Pharisee's Table

In Jesus' day, people usually did not sit on chairs while they ate a meal. They sat on the floor, perhaps on cushions, around a low table, with their feet to the side or behind them (Brown et al., *Beholding Salvation*, 48).

Jesus Calms the Storm

Sea of Galilee

The Sea of Galilee is more a lake than a sea. It is pear-shaped, and the Jordan River flows through it. Located lower than sea level, it is about twelve miles long and seven miles wide. In the Old Testament, it is called the Sea of Chinnereth, and in the New Testament it is sometimes called the Lake of Gennesaret (Bible Dictionary, 677).

"Master, the Tempest Is Raging"

Hymn number 105 in the Latter-day Saint hymnbook retells the story of Jesus calming the Sea of Galilee. It describes not only the peace that Jesus brought to the water but also the peace our souls feel as we come unto Jesus and replace our fears with faith in him.

Jesus spent much time in the land around the Sea of Galilee. Multitudes of people followed him and sought for his blessing. Jesus did not really have a home there—or anywhere. He went from place to place, teaching and helping the people.

One day he and his apostles boarded a ship and set off for the other side of the Sea of Galilee. As they sailed across the sea, a strong wind began to blow, and waves crashed around them. The storm raged on until the waves were so high that they covered the boat.

The apostles were filled with fear that they might die in the storm, but Jesus was sound asleep. Finally, the apostles woke Jesus and begged him to save them. He asked them why they were afraid and why they did not have more faith.

Then Jesus stood and commanded the wind and the sea to be still. Immediately, the wind stopped blowing, and the sea was calm. Jesus' apostles marveled at his great power. They exclaimed, "What manner of man is this, that even the winds and the sea obey him!" It was a testimony that Jesus is the Son of God.

*Whether the wrath of the
  storm-tossed sea
Or demons or men or
  whatever it be,
No waters can swallow
  the ship where lies
The Master of ocean and
  earth and skies.
They all shall sweetly
  obey thy will:
Peace, be still; peace,
  be still.*

Jesus Casts Out Evil Spirits

Fetters

Fetters are metal bands that are placed around the ankles of prisoners to keep them from escaping.

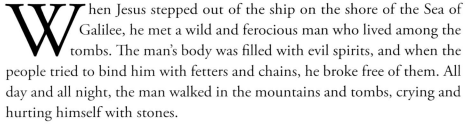

When Jesus stepped out of the ship on the shore of the Sea of Galilee, he met a wild and ferocious man who lived among the tombs. The man's body was filled with evil spirits, and when the people tried to bind him with fetters and chains, he broke free of them. All day and all night, the man walked in the mountains and tombs, crying and hurting himself with stones.

While he was still far away, the wild man saw Jesus and ran to him. At first, the man worshipped Jesus, and then he cried with a loud voice and pled with Jesus not to hurt him. Jesus commanded the evil spirit to leave the man. When Jesus asked the name of the evil spirit, the man answered, "Legion," meaning there were many evil spirits who had power over him.

The evil spirits pled with Jesus not to send them away. Not far off, a herd of about two thousand pigs were grazing near the mountain. The evil spirits begged Jesus to send them into the bodies of the pigs. They would rather possess the pigs' bodies than have no bodies at all. As soon as the evil spirits entered the pigs, the pigs ran violently down a steep hill and into the sea. They choked in the water and drowned.

Swine

According to Jewish law, swine, or pigs, were considered to be unclean, meaning that the Jews were forbidden to eat them. It was against the law for Jews to buy and sell pigs, and they were offended that people were raising pigs in their country (McConkie, *DNTC* 1:313).

The men who were in charge of feeding the pigs told everyone in the city and the countryside what had happened. They all went to see Jesus and the man who had been filled with evil spirits. The man who had once been wild was now sitting peacefully and was thinking clearly. The men from the city were frightened. They did not understand how the power of God could heal the wild man. They asked Jesus to go away.

Jesus entered the ship again, and the newly healed man asked Jesus if he could go with him. Jesus told him to go home to his friends and tell them how the Lord had had compassion on him and what great things the Lord had done for him.

The man did what Jesus told him to do. He went throughout Decapolis, telling his story, and the people were amazed at all the things he told them.

Jesus Feeds Thousands

Death of John the Baptist

King Herod was so pleased with the beautiful dancer Salome that he promised to give her anything she wanted. The girl's mother, Herod's wife, hated John the Baptist because he had told her to repent. She instructed her daughter to ask for John's head. Herod honored Salome's request and had the prophet killed (Bible Dictionary, 768).

King Herod put John the Baptist in prison and then had him put to death. When Jesus heard this news, he left in a ship to find a place where he could be away from the crowds of people. But when the people heard where Jesus went, they followed him, bringing their sick and afflicted with them. When Jesus saw the multitudes, he felt compassion for them. All day long, Jesus taught the people and healed those who were sick.

When evening came, the apostles suggested that Jesus send the crowds away so they could go to the villages and buy food before it was too late in the day. Jesus replied that the people did not need to leave. He asked if anyone had brought food. A boy offered to share his five loaves of bread and two fishes.

Jesus commanded the crowd of people to sit on the grass. He took the five loaves of bread and two fishes and looked up to heaven. He thanked Heavenly Father for the food and blessed it. Then Jesus broke the food into pieces and gave it to his apostles to serve to the people.

The apostles served the bread and fish to the multitude until everyone was filled. When they gathered the food that remained, there were still twelve baskets full of bread and fish. With only two fishes and five loaves of bread, Jesus had miraculously fed five thousand men, plus women and children!

On another occasion, the people had listened to Jesus teach outside the villages for three days. There was nothing for them to eat, and Jesus had compassion on them. He did not want to send them away hungry, so he asked his apostles how much food there was among them. They had seven loaves of bread and a few little fishes.

Again, Jesus commanded the crowd of people to sit on the ground. He took the bread and fish, thanked Heavenly Father for them, blessed them, and broke them into pieces. Just as before, the bread and fish were served to all the people. When everyone had had enough to eat, the apostles gathered seven baskets full of food that remained. On that day, Jesus fed more than four thousand men, in addition to women and children, with only seven loaves of bread and a few fishes. It was another miracle!

Counting the People

During the time of Jesus, record keepers counted only the men in the crowd. If Jesus fed five thousand *men,* he may have fed at least twice that number all together.

卌 卌 卌 卌 卌 卌
卌 卌 卌 卌 卌 卌
卌 卌 卌 卌 卌 卌
卌 卌 ||

Jesus Blesses the Children

Children of the Kingdom

During the week before Jesus was crucified, he cast the moneychangers out of the temple, and he healed the blind and the lame who came to him there. In the Bible, Matthew wrote that on this occasion, the "children" in the temple praised Jesus, saying, "Hosanna to the Son of David!" (Matthew 21:12–16). Joseph Smith clarified this scripture, telling us that these were "children of the kingdom," people who believed in Jesus Christ, not necessarily those who were young in age (Ogden and Skinner, *Gospels,* 475).

While Jesus and his apostles were walking home to Capernaum, the apostles began to disagree with each other about which of them would be the greatest or most important. When they reached the place they were going to stay, Jesus called the twelve apostles together. He sat down and taught them that it is better to be humble and to serve others than it is to try to become important. He called a little child to him and set him in the middle of them. Jesus told the apostles that those who become humble like a little child will be the greatest in the kingdom of heaven. He told them that unless they had faith like little children, they would not even enter the kingdom of heaven. He taught them that if someone welcomes and cares for a little child in Jesus' name, that person shows that he or she loves and cares about Jesus, too.

Jesus warned his apostles that if anyone injures or sets a bad example for a little child, it would be better for that person if he were drowned in the deep sea. Jesus cautioned them not to think they were better than little children or to be scornful of them. He explained that the angels from heaven watch over little children.

On another occasion, some parents brought their young children to Jesus, hoping he would bless them. But Jesus' apostles scolded the parents for bringing their children to him. When Jesus saw what was happening, he told his apostles to allow the little children to come to him and not to stop them. He told his apostles that those who hope to enter the kingdom of God need to be like little children. He took the children into his arms and blessed them. Jesus loved the little children.

Capernaum

Capernaum, one of the largest towns near the Sea of Galilee, was like Jesus' hometown during the time of his public ministry. Peter's home was in Capernaum, and perhaps the child that Jesus called into his arms was Peter's child (McConkie, *DNTC* 1:415; Holzapfel et. al., *World,* 116).

Jesus Walks on Water

Another Miracle in the Sea of Galilee

The Jewish priests collected money from the people, like a tax or tribute, to pay for temple expenses. In Capernaum, a city near the Sea of Galilee, the priests asked Peter if Jesus would pay the tribute money. Peter said that he would pay. When Peter went into the house, Jesus talked with him about the tribute. He told Peter to go to the Sea of Galilee and cast a hook into the water. Inside the mouth of the first fish he caught, Peter would find a piece of money. Peter did as Jesus told him. Miraculously, the money was there in the fish's mouth, and Peter used it to pay the tribute (Matthew 17:24–27; Talmage, *Jesus the Christ,* 382–85).

After miraculously feeding the multitude, Jesus sent his apostles ahead of him in a ship to the other side of the Sea of Galilee. He stayed behind until it was time to send the people back to their homes. Then he went alone into a mountain to pray.

The ship carrying his apostles was tossed by waves and a strong wind. When evening came, they were in the middle of the sea, some distance away from the shore. During the "fourth watch," in the middle of the night, Jesus went down the mountain and began walking on the water toward the ship.

The apostles were afraid when they saw him. They did not know it was Jesus. Thinking he was a spirit, they cried out with fear. Immediately, Jesus reassured them. "Be of good cheer," he said. "It is I. Be not afraid."

Wanting to be certain, Peter answered him, "Lord, if it is you, invite me to come unto you on the water." Jesus invited him to come. Peter left the ship and started walking on the water toward Jesus! Suddenly, he

remembered the wind and the waves, and he was afraid. He started to sink into the water, and he cried out, "Lord, save me."

Jesus stretched out his hand. Catching Peter, he asked him why he had doubted. When Jesus and Peter were safely in the boat, the wind stopped. The apostles fell at Jesus' feet and worshipped him, declaring that they knew he was the Son of God.

Fourth Watch

The Romans divided the night into four "watches," or turns, when one person would watch over the others while they slept. The fourth watch was between three o'clock and six o'clock in the morning (Matthew 14:25a; Bible Dictionary, 788).

Jesus Raises the Dead

Burial

Natural caves were often used as gravesites, especially for wealthy people. A Jewish burial usually took place on the day the person died. The body was treated with spices and covered in linen cloths, with a square of linen wrapped around the head, before the body was placed inside the cave (Talmage, *Jesus the Christ*, 494).

Jesus Restores Life

Besides Lazarus, Jesus brought at least two other people back to life. When the only son of a widow died, Jesus called the young man back from the dead (Luke 7:11–17). And when Jairus, a ruler of the synagogue, sought for Jesus after his twelve-year-old daughter died, Jesus restored the girl to life (Luke 8:41–42).

Jesus' good friends Mary, Martha, and their brother, Lazarus, lived in Bethany. When Lazarus became deathly ill, the two sisters sent for Jesus. When he received the message, Jesus did not rush to Lazarus's bedside. He stayed where he was for two days before starting for Bethany. Because the Jews had tried to stone Jesus the last time he had been near that town, his apostles were afraid it was not safe for Jesus to travel there. But Jesus told them that he knew Lazarus was dead and that he needed to go and wake him from his "sleep."

When Jesus and the apostles arrived in Bethany, Lazarus had been dead four days. Mary and Martha's neighbors had gathered to comfort them. When Martha heard that Jesus was coming, she went to meet him, but Mary stayed in the house. Martha found Jesus and shared her sorrow with him. She said she knew that if he had been there, her brother would not have died. But she also knew that God would grant whatever Jesus asked of him. Jesus assured Martha that her brother would rise again—and that whoever believed in Jesus would have everlasting life. Martha declared that she knew that Jesus was the Christ, the Son of God whom prophets said would come into the world.

Martha ran to tell Mary that Jesus wanted to see her. Mary arose quickly and went to meet him just outside the town. The people who had come to comfort the sisters followed her. Mary fell at Jesus' feet and cried, saying that she, too, believed that if Jesus had been there, Lazarus would not have died.

When Jesus saw Mary and their friends weeping, he was filled with sorrow, and he wept, too. The people remarked that Jesus must have loved Lazarus very much. Jesus asked them to show him where Lazarus was buried. Jesus moaned within himself when he came to Lazarus's grave, a cave with a stone over its opening. When Jesus asked for the stone to be moved, Martha reminded him that Lazarus had been dead for four days and that his body probably had started to smell. Jesus, in turn, reminded Martha to believe, and she would see the glory of God.

When the stone had been removed, Jesus looked toward heaven. He thanked Heavenly Father for hearing his prayers. He wanted the people to know that he had been sent from God. Then, with a loud voice, Jesus cried, "Lazarus, come forth."

Lazarus walked out of the cave! His hands and feet were still wrapped in his burial clothes, and a napkin was around his face. Jesus told the people to loosen the wrappings so Lazarus could move freely. Lazarus was alive again! Many of those who witnessed this miracle believed in Jesus ever after.

The Good Shepherd

Sheepfold

A sheepfold is a pen or corral for holding sheep. In ancient times, many sheepfolds were made of drystone stacked high enough to keep the sheep from escaping. The sheepfold helped the shepherd keep his flock safe from predators, especially during the night.

Jesus called himself the good shepherd. He did not mean that he took care of animals. He used the example of how a shepherd lovingly cares for his sheep to explain his relationship with all of God's children. Jesus explained that a shepherd enters the sheepfold through the door. The doorkeeper of the sheepfold knows the shepherd and welcomes him when he comes. But a thief or a robber sneaks into the pen or climbs up some other way. The sheep recognize the voice of the true shepherd and follow him. They will not follow a stranger's voice. In the same way, those who believe in Jesus recognize his voice. They know him, love him, and choose to follow him.

Jesus taught that he is not only the good shepherd but he is also the door to the sheepfold. In other words, only through Jesus can God's children be saved and enter the kingdom of God. Thieves may try to steal or kill, but Jesus comes to make life better for all of God's children, to give them life after death and the possibility of eternal life, which means to live with God forever.

Jesus told his followers a parable, or a short story that teaches a lesson, about a shepherd who had one hundred sheep. One of his sheep was lost, so the shepherd left the ninety-nine sheep safe in the pen and searched the mountains for the one that was lost. He looked for the sheep until he found it, and then he carried it home on his shoulders. The shepherd called his friends and neighbors to come and rejoice with him because he had found his lost sheep. Jesus taught that, in the same way, our Heavenly Father rejoices whenever one of His children repents and returns to Him.

Jesus told his disciples in the Holy Land that he had sheep in another "fold," or, in other words, he had people to teach in other parts of the world. Jesus is the shepherd of the whole earth. He loves his children everywhere and wants them all to hear his gospel.

The Middle Eastern Shepherd

In his teachings about the good shepherd, Jesus described the kind of shepherd who loves and cares for his sheep. The shepherd knows each one, he names each one, and his sheep know him and recognize his voice. Shepherds in the Holy Land traditionally care for their sheep in this way. Even if the sheep are kept in a fold with other flocks, each sheep knows its own shepherd and follows him out of the pen (Proctor and Proctor, *Source,* 126).

The Ten Lepers

Jews and Samaritans

Jews considered Samaritans to be strangers and even enemies. Anciently, when the Assyrians conquered the northern kingdom of Israel, the Jews who remained in Samaria mixed with other people, married them, and adopted their religion. The Jews in Jesus' day felt that they were better than the Samaritans because the Samaritans no longer practiced the true religion (Bible Dictionary, 768). When the apostles taught them the gospel of Jesus Christ, however, many Samaritans accepted it. There are a few Samaritan communities in modern-day Israel.

On his way toward Jerusalem, Jesus passed through Samaria and Galilee. As he entered a certain village, Jesus met ten men who suffered from a disease called leprosy that ate away their skin and made them very miserable. The law said that, in order to keep the disease from spreading, the lepers must stay away from other people. Because they could not get close to him, the ten men called out to Jesus, "Master, have mercy on us."

When Jesus realized the men suffered from leprosy, he told them to go and show themselves to the priests. According to the law of Moses, lepers who had been healed were required to go to the priests for a ceremonial offering and cleansing. Jesus was asking these men to exercise faith by going to the priests even before they had been healed. Miraculously, as they obeyed and were on their way to see the priests, the men were healed.

When one of the lepers—a Samaritan—saw that his leprosy was gone, he turned back and praised God with a loud voice. He fell down at Jesus' feet and thanked him. Jesus asked where the other nine lepers were. Only the Samaritan, a stranger among the Jews, had returned to give thanks. Jesus told the man to arise and go on his way because his faith had made him whole.

Ceremonial Cleansing of Lepers

According to Jewish law, if a leper were healed, he went to the priest, and the priest made an offering to the Lord for him. The healed person then washed his clothes, shaved all of his hair, and washed himself. After seven days, the priest made another offering in his behalf as a way of giving thanks to God that the person had been cleansed (Leviticus 14:2–20).

The Rich Young Man

One day, a rich young man came running to see Jesus. He knelt before Jesus and asked, "What shall I do that I may inherit eternal life?" He wanted to know how to be worthy to live with Heavenly Father again.

The young man seemed to be sincere. He was not trying to trick Jesus as the Pharisees sometimes tried to do. Jesus answered by telling him to keep the commandments: He should not love another man's wife; he should not kill, steal, or lie; and he should honor his parents. The young man told Jesus he had kept all of those commandments since his youth.

Jesus told the young man that he lacked only one thing to be worthy before the Lord: He must be willing to sell all that he had and give the money to the poor. Then he would have treasure in heaven.

The young man walked away feeling sad. He owned many valuable things, and it would be very hard for him to give them up.

The Widow's Mite

The Jewish priests placed chests in the temple to receive the people's offerings of money to the Lord. The money was used by the priests to care for the temple and to care for the poor. Some people deposited large amounts of money in the treasury. They seemed to want other people to notice how much they gave. Others placed their offerings there quietly.

As Jesus sat near the treasury one day, a poor widow tossed two mites into the chest. When Jesus saw what she had done, he called his disciples to gather around him. He explained to them that even though two mites was not very much money, this poor widow had given more than any of the other people in the temple that day. The rich gave a lot of money, but they kept even more for themselves. This poor woman had given not just the money that was left after she took care of her own needs but she gave everything she had. She gave willingly and with love, trusting that God would bless her.

Temple Treasury

The temple treasury consisted of thirteen chests in which people might deposit their offerings of money, like our tithing and fast offerings today. Each chest had a trumpet-shaped receptacle and was labeled according to what the money would be used for (Talmage, *Jesus the Christ,* 561).

Mites

In terms of today's money, a mite was worth about half a penny.

The Story of the Talents

Talent

In the ancient world, a talent was a unit of money equal to about 75 pounds of gold or silver (Ogden and Skinner, *Gospels*, 777).

To help his followers understand how to be worthy of the kingdom of heaven, Jesus told a story about a man who traveled to a country far away. Before the man left, he gave each of his servants some talents, or money, according to their ability to use them. To one servant, he gave five talents. To another servant, he gave two talents. And to another, he gave one talent. The man left on his journey, and his servants used their talents in different ways.

The servant who was given five talents went to the market and traded until he had earned five more talents. He now had ten. The servant who was given two talents also doubled the amount of his money. He now had four talents. But the servant who was given one talent buried it in the earth.

After a long time, the master returned and asked his servants to account for what they had done with the talents he had given them. When the servant who was given five talents reported that he had earned five more, the master said, "Well done, thou good and faithful servant." He also praised the servant who increased his talents from two to four. But with the servant who buried his talent the master was not pleased. He told the servant that he had been wicked and lazy, and the master took away that servant's talent and gave it to the servant who had ten.

When we put our talents and abilities to good use, the Lord will be pleased with us. If we give our best effort to increase our abilities and reach our potential, the Lord will reward us. But if we bury our talents and do not try, we will lose our talents, and we will not become all that the Lord would have us be.

The Story of the Ten Young Women

To help his followers understand how to be prepared to enter the kingdom of heaven, Jesus told a story about ten young women who were attending a wedding, waiting for the bridegroom to come. Five of the young women were wise—they brought extra oil for their lamps. But five of the young women were foolish—they brought no extra oil.

All of the young women fell asleep. At midnight, they were awakened and warned that the bridegroom would soon be there. The lamps of the foolish young women had gone out, so they went to the market to buy more oil. While they were gone, the bridegroom came. The wise young women whose lamps were still burning were permitted to come into the house for the wedding. But when the foolish young women came back, they found the door shut, and they were not allowed inside.

Just as the wise young women in this story were prepared to meet the bridegroom, we must prepare ourselves and be spiritually ready when Jesus comes to earth again.

Oil Lamps

Oil lamps used in Jesus' time had an opening in the center for pouring in oil and a hole in the end for the wick. Oil in the lamp burned for about three hours at a time (Hastings, *Children's*, 252).

The Story of the Good Samaritan

Levites

Levites were priests in ancient Israel. Because they assisted other priests in the temple, we might think of them as being similar in some ways to modern-day temple workers (Bible Dictionary, 724).

A lawyer asked Jesus what he needed to do to inherit eternal life. Jesus answered that the man needed to obey the commandments to love God and to love his neighbor. When the lawyer asked, "Who is my neighbor?" Jesus told him a story.

A man who was traveling from Jerusalem to Jericho fell among thieves who robbed him, wounded him, and left him on the road, half dead. A priest saw the man on the road, but he did not stop to help him. Likewise, a Levite looked at the wounded man and passed by on the other side of the road. But when a Samaritan—an enemy of the Jews—saw the wounded man, he stopped to care for him. He cleaned and bandaged the man's wounds and carried him on his donkey to an inn. The Samaritan even paid the innkeeper to feed and care for the wounded man.

Jesus asked the lawyer which of the three men was the wounded man's "neighbor." The lawyer said it was the merciful and kind Samaritan who acted like a true neighbor to the wounded man. Jesus told the lawyer to go and be kind to others as the Samaritan had done.

Good neighbors love and help each other. This story teaches that we need to be loving and consider all of God's children to be our "neighbors," even if we do not know them or live near them.

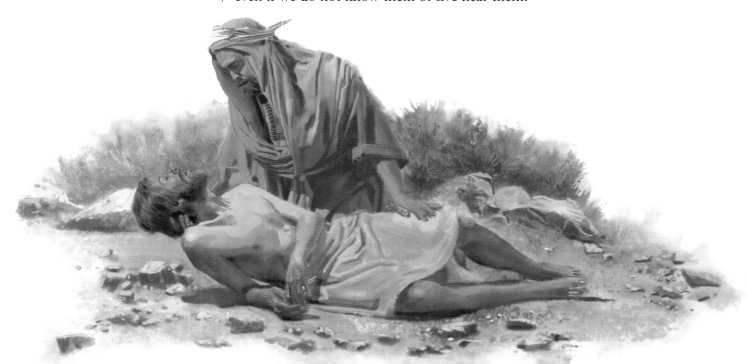

The Story of the Sower

A group of people were gathered by the Sea of Galilee, listening to Jesus' teachings. He told a parable, or story, about a sower, or a man who planted seeds. Some of the seeds the man planted fell to the side of the path, and the birds came and ate them. Some of the seeds fell into stony places where they could not grow. Other seeds fell among thorny plants that choked the seedlings. But some of the seeds fell onto good ground, where they flourished and brought forth much fruit.

Jesus' apostles asked him why he used parables to teach the people. Jesus explained that those who had humble and teachable spirits would understand the meaning of the parables. In this story, for example, the seeds represent the word of God, and the places where the seeds fall represent the hearts of those who hear the word. The word cannot grow in hearts that are hard like stone. But when people hear the word of God and accept the gospel of Jesus Christ, their testimonies can grow in the fertile soil, or "good ground," of gospel living. The word of God in their lives will flower and grow into the fruits of peace, joy, purpose, and love.

Like a Mustard Seed

In another parable, Jesus compared the kingdom of heaven to a mustard seed, which grows into a great tree, and birds want to make their nests in it. In the same way, people will flock to the gospel of Jesus Christ and want to be part of His Church (Matthew 13:31–32).

The Story of the Prodigal Son

Parables

A parable is a story that teaches a lesson. In a parable, objects or events in everyday life are compared to gospel principles. Parables help us understand gospel truths (Parry and Parry, *Parables,* xi-xii).

"Husks the Pigs Ate"

The husks the pigs ate were most likely leathery brown pods from the carob tree. A common food for livestock in the Middle East, carob pods contain seeds that look like beans (Ogden, *Where Jesus Walked,* 99).

Some of the Jews complained because Jesus spoke and even ate with people who had sinned. Jesus told them three parables, or stories, to help them understand that every soul is of great worth to God.

The first parable was about a shepherd who owned a hundred sheep. When one of the sheep was lost, the shepherd was worried because he knew that sheep cannot defend themselves against the wolves and lions of the desert. The shepherd left his ninety-nine other sheep to look for the one that was lost. When he found it, he laid it on his shoulders and carried it home. The shepherd called his friends and neighbors to rejoice with him because he had found the one that was lost.

The second parable told of a woman who had ten pieces of silver. When she lost one piece of silver, she lit a candle and swept her house, searching for the lost coin. When at last she found it, she called her friends and neighbors to rejoice with her.

The third parable was longer. It told of a father and his two sons. The younger son asked his father to give him his share of the father's money and possessions. The father divided his property between the two sons, and the younger one took what was his and journeyed to a place far away. He spent everything he had, wasting his time and money on riotous living.

A famine spread throughout the land, and the younger son was desperate for food. He found a job feeding pigs, and he was so hungry he would have eaten the husks the pigs ate. Truly humble and sincerely sorry for what he had done, the younger son decided to return home. He no longer felt worthy to be known as his father's son, but he thought that perhaps he could work as his father's servant.

From a great distance away, the father saw his son coming, and he ran to meet him. He hugged his son, kissed him, and welcomed him home. The father told his servants to give his son the best robe, a ring, and new shoes to wear. He also ordered his finest calf to be killed and prepared for a feast to celebrate his son's return.

The older son had remained at home, working hard on his father's land and serving his father well. When he came in from the field that day, he heard music and dancing. When he learned what had happened, he was angry and did not want to attend the celebration. His father came looking for him. The older son complained that even though he had always been faithful and obedient, his father had never given a feast in his honor. The father assured this son that he would always be in his father's favor and that he would be given everything the father had. But it was right for them to celebrate the younger brother's return. It was as if the young man had died and was now alive again. The son who had been lost was now found, and the father loved him.

These three parables show that the worth of souls is great to our Father in Heaven. No matter how "lost" his sons and daughters may be, Heavenly Father and Jesus love them and rejoice when they "come home."

The Triumphal Entry of Jesus into Jerusalem

Hosanna

Hosanna is a Hebrew word that means "save us now." During the ancient Feast of Tabernacles, Jewish people waved palm branches and cried "Hosanna!" to celebrate their ancestors' deliverance from Egypt (Bible Dictionary, 704–5). In modern times, the Hosanna Shout is performed at temple dedications by waving white handkerchiefs instead of palm branches (lds.org, *Guide to the Scriptures*).

Once again it was spring, and the Jews were gathering to Jerusalem to celebrate the Feast of the Passover. People had come from near and far to make sacrifices in the temple and to prepare for the important holiday.

Jesus was staying in Bethany with his friends Lazarus, Martha, and Mary. Five days before Passover, he left Bethany to go to Jerusalem for the feast. He sent his apostles to a nearby village to find a young donkey colt that had never before been ridden and bring the donkey to him. He instructed them that if anyone were to ask them why they were taking the colt, they should explain that the Lord needed it. When the colt was brought to Jesus, he mounted it and began to ride into the crowded city, with his apostles and other followers walking beside him.

Ancient prophets had foretold that the King of the Jews would come to Jerusalem riding a young donkey. When word spread that Jesus was

riding into Jerusalem, the Pharisees were afraid that, because of him, they would lose their power. They knew of the miracles Jesus had performed, and they were fearful that the people would look to Jesus as their leader. They made plans to have Jesus killed. But many others watched for Jesus to enter the city so they could honor and worship him.

When Jesus rode through the city gates, the crowds of believers welcomed him to Jerusalem. Laying their robes and tree branches like a carpet across the road, they ran to meet him, waving branches from palm trees and calling out, "Hosanna! Blessed is he that cometh in the name of the Lord! Hosanna in the highest!"

When Jesus reached the temple, he dismounted from the donkey. He went into the temple and, as he had done several years before, overthrew the tables where people were buying and selling things. He ordered them out of the temple grounds, declaring again that the temple was a house of prayer and not a den of thieves. Then he healed those who were blind and lame, and his followers once again sang out, "Hosanna to the Son of David!"

Mary Anoints Jesus

Before Jesus left his friends' home in Bethany, Mary performed an act of great honor, worship, and affection for him. With a pound of spikenard, a very expensive and precious ointment, she anointed Jesus' feet and then wiped them with her hair. Jesus said that she had done this to prepare him for his burial later that week (John 12:1–9; Ogden and Skinner, *Gospels,* 458–59, 542–43).

The Last Supper

Eating without Utensils

Jesus and his apostles most likely ate the Passover meal without using forks, knives, or spoons. The custom at the time was to dip flat pieces of bread into bowls of food, using the bread as a sort of spoon or scoop (*Life and Teachings* manual, 160).

As the Passover drew near, Jesus asked Peter and John to prepare a place for him and the other apostles to eat the special feast. He told them that when they entered Jerusalem, they would meet a man carrying a pitcher of water. They were to follow the man to his home and ask him to lead them to a guest chamber where the Master might eat the Passover meal with his apostles. Jesus said the man would show them a large upper room furnished with the things they would need.

Soon everything was prepared for the Passover meal. The feast that night would later be known as the Last Supper because it was the final meal Jesus would eat in mortality. As he sat with his twelve apostles that evening, Jesus told them that he knew one of them would betray him to wicked men who wanted to kill him. The apostles became very distressed. Each one asked him, "Lord, is it I?" Jesus knew that Judas Iscariot had already agreed with the chief priests to betray him into their hands in exchange for thirty pieces of silver. When Judas asked, "Is it I?" Jesus responded, "Thou hast said."

During the evening, the apostles began to disagree with each other about who among them was the greatest. Jesus taught them an important lesson. He asked them to tell who is greater—the person sitting down to eat or the person who serves the meal. He answered his own question by reminding them that Jesus himself had come to be the servant of all of God's children, and then he set an example for them of what it means to be a humble servant. After supper, he took a towel, poured water in a basin, and, one by one, he washed the apostles' feet, something that only a servant would do.

At the Last Supper, Jesus introduced the sacrament. He took bread, blessed it, and broke it into pieces. He gave the broken bread to his apostles, telling them it would help them to remember his body, which he would give as a sacrifice. And then he took a cup of wine, blessed it, and gave it to the apostles to drink. It would help them remember his blood, which would be shed for the sins of men. When they partook of the sacrament after his death, they were to eat and drink reverently, remembering Jesus and his great sacrifice for the world.

Finally, Jesus gave them "a new commandment." He told them that they should love one another as Jesus had loved them. This is how people would recognize Jesus' disciples—by the loving way they treated other people.

Jesus and his apostles sang a hymn together. Night had fallen, and they walked to the Mount of Olives.

Paschal Lamb

At Passover time, Jewish families sacrificed a "paschal" lamb, a firstborn male lamb without any imperfections. Jesus Christ was the fulfillment of this symbol. He truly was the Lamb of God, who offered his perfect life to enable all of God's children to live again (OT student manual 1:117).

In the Garden of Gethsemane

After the Passover meal, Jesus and his apostles left the upper room and walked to an orchard of olive trees in a garden called Gethsemane. He asked the apostles to stay where they were and to watch and pray. Wanting to be alone, Jesus moved a short distance away from his apostles—about as far as a person could throw a stone.

As Jesus prayed, he began to feel sad and very troubled. He asked his Father in Heaven if there were any way he could be spared from the suffering he was about to endure. But he also prayed, "Thy will be done."

A short while later, Jesus returned to his apostles, only to find them asleep. He asked them, "Could ye not watch with me one hour?" But he understood their weariness. A second time, he went away to pray by himself and then returned to his apostles, who again had fallen asleep.

A third time, Jesus prayed. He was in great pain, and his feelings were so strong and powerful that drops of blood came, like sweat, from every pore of his body. An angel appeared from heaven to strengthen and comfort him.

Jesus had chosen to do what his Heavenly Father wanted him to do. He chose to bear the great suffering of every person's sin, pain, and sorrow. He was the Savior of the world.

When Jesus' prayer and suffering were over at last, he once again returned to his apostles. He told them that the time had come for him to be betrayed into the hands of wicked men. In the distance, they could see men with torches, swords, and staves coming toward them, with Judas Iscariot in the lead.

Judas walked up to Jesus and kissed him on the cheek. Jesus knew that this was the sign of Judas's betrayal. In exchange for thirty pieces of silver, Judas had agreed to show those who were with him who Jesus was by giving him a kiss. Jesus fully understood what was taking place, and he did not resist when the guards took him.

Not ready to give Jesus over to the wicked men, Peter drew his sword and cut off the ear of the high priest's servant. Jesus immediately stopped Peter and told him to put away his sword. He warned Peter, "They that take the sword shall perish with the sword." Then Jesus touched the servant's ear and healed him. Jesus reminded Peter and the others that, at any time, he could ask his Heavenly Father to send twelve legions of angels or more to protect him. But he knew that the scriptures must be fulfilled. Jesus was willing to give up his mortal life so that all of Heavenly Father's children could have eternal life. Jesus did not stop the wicked men from leading him away.

Gethsemane

Gethsemane, the name of the garden where Jesus prayed, means "oil press." Filled with olive trees, the garden was also the place where olives were pressed to produce oil for lamps, food, and lotions.

Staves

Staves are long, strong sticks that are used for many things. A staff might be used as a walking stick, for support in traveling over rough roads, or it might be a tool for use in herding sheep or a weapon used in self-defense (Ogden and Skinner, *Gospels,* 162).

The Trial of Jesus

Sanhedrin

The Sanhedrin, the highest Jewish court, had seventy-one members who were chief priests, scribes, and elders. They administered both religious and political laws for the Jews (Ogden and Skinner, *Gospels,* 753–54).

"Destroy This Temple"

When Jesus said, "Destroy this temple, and in three days I will raise it up," he was speaking of the "temple" of his own body, prophesying about his death and resurrection (John 2:18–22). The false witnesses at his trial twisted Jesus' words to give them a different and incorrect meaning.

During the middle of the night, the soldiers and others who had arrested Jesus brought him before the Jewish council, the Sanhedrin, to be judged. Before the trial even began, the leaders in the Sanhedrin had decided that Jesus must die. But first, they needed to accuse him of a crime. Because Jesus had never done anything wrong, witnesses must be found who would lie and change the meaning of Jesus' words. Then the leaders would have an excuse to have Jesus put to death.

Jesus was taken before Annas, a leader in the Sanhedrin. When Jesus did not answer their questions in the way they wanted, one of the officers hit him with the palm of his hand. Annas sent Jesus, bound with cords, to appear before Caiaphas, the high priest. The scribes and elders gathered in the high priest's palace for the trial. False witnesses were brought to testify against Jesus, but none of them agreed with each other. At last, two came forward who both said they heard Jesus say he could destroy the temple and rebuild it in three days. Finally, Caiaphas asked Jesus if he were the Christ, the Son of God. Jesus answered, "Thou hast said." Caiaphas immediately tore his coat to show his strong objection to Jesus' words. The Sanhedrin convicted Jesus of blasphemy, a great offense toward God. The Jewish leaders spat in Jesus' face, pushed him, hit him, and led him away to the Roman governor Pilate, who had the authority to put Jesus to death.

Pilate asked the chief priests and elders why they had brought Jesus to him. They said it was because Jesus wanted to be king of the Jews, hoping this would give Pilate reason to have Jesus killed. Pilate questioned Jesus in the judgment hall, but he could not find that Jesus had committed any crime. Pilate's wife had a dream about Jesus, and she knew that he was an innocent man. She warned Pilate not to harm him. When Pilate heard that Jesus was from Galilee, he sent him to Herod, governor of that region, who was in Jerusalem at that time.

Herod questioned Jesus, but Jesus would not answer him. The Jewish leaders shouted questions and accusations at Jesus, but he remained silent. Herod and his soldiers mocked Jesus, put a rich robe over his shoulders, and sent him back to Pilate.

It was a custom at Passover time for the governor to release one prisoner of the people's choice. Pilate offered to release Jesus, but the Jews demanded that Jesus be crucified. Finally, Pilate washed his hands in front of the people to show that he did not want to take responsibility for Jesus' death. In the end, he did not want to oppose the shouting crowd of Jews. He ordered Jesus to be crucified.

Blasphemy

Blasphemy is to speak or act very rudely or with great irreverence toward God. The punishment for blasphemy was to be stoned to death. But Jesus was crucified, rather than stoned, as he himself had prophesied (John 3:14; Talmage, *Jesus the Christ,* 632–33).

The Crucifixion of Jesus

The Cross

A cross that was used for crucifixion had two parts: a strong, vertical piece of wood 8 or 9 feet tall and a movable crosspiece that was carried by the accused to the place of crucifixion (*Life and Teachings* manual, 184).

Simon of Cyrene

The Roman soldiers ordered a man named Simon to help carry Jesus' cross. Simon was from a Jewish colony called Cyrene, in Libya, on the northern coast of Africa. Mark's Gospel suggests that Simon's family became followers of Christ (Talmage, *Jesus the Christ,* 666).

When the clamoring crowd demanded that Jesus be crucified, Pilate delivered him to the Roman soldiers, who took him into the palace and stripped him of his outer clothing. After they had cruelly whipped him, they put the purple robe back on his shoulders and placed a reed in his hand and a crown of thorns on his head. They mockingly bowed and jeered at the "king," spitting on him and slapping him. Once again, Pilate brought Jesus before the crowd, saying, "I find no fault in him." Once again, the chief priests and the officers cried out, "Crucify him!"

The soldiers took the robe off Jesus' shoulders and led him away, along with two criminals who had been convicted of stealing. The soldiers caused Jesus to carry his own wooden cross. Weak and tired from the suffering he had already endured, Jesus walked slowly. The soldiers became impatient and ordered another man to help him carry the cross. People gathered to watch, and women wept as Jesus passed by. He spoke to them, prophesying of hard days ahead for the people of Jerusalem.

They arrived at Golgotha, the place outside the gates of the city where people who were convicted of a crime were crucified. The crowd gathered around, some of them mocking Jesus, others overcome with grief as they watched the soldiers pound spikes, or long nails, through Jesus' hands and feet and into the cross. The soldiers lifted the heavy cross into place and kept guard over those who had been hung there to die.

While he was on the cross, Jesus prayed for the Roman soldiers, saying, "Father, forgive them, for they know not what they do." As the Psalmist had foretold, the soldiers divided Jesus' clothing among themselves. Because they all wanted his coat, they cast lots as a way of choosing which of them received the coat.

Jesus looked down from the cross and saw his mother, Mary. He spoke to his disciple John, asking him to take care of Mary as if she were his own mother. From that hour forward, John took Mary into his home and cared for her.

At noon, the sun turned dark, and there was darkness over the land for three hours. In agony, Jesus cried out to Heavenly Father. Then, knowing that he had completed everything that he had come to earth to do, Jesus said, "It is finished." And he allowed himself to die.

A violent earthquake erupted, and rocks fell and broke apart. The veil of the temple tore in half, from top to bottom. Seeing these things, the centurion in charge of the soldiers exclaimed, "Truly this was the Son of God."

The Psalmist

In Psalm 22, King David used language that foretold many of the things that would happen during the Savior's crucifixion, including the piercing of his hands and feet (Psalm 22:16) and the soldiers dividing Jesus' clothing among them (Psalm 22:18).

Destruction in the New World

Chapter 8 of 3 Nephi records the tempests, earthquakes, fires, winds, and darkness that took place on the American continent during Jesus' crucifixion. After the destruction, the darkness there lasted for three days (3 Nephi 8:20–23).

The Resurrection of Jesus

Jewish Sabbath

The Jewish Sabbath, or holy day of rest, begins at sundown on Friday and continues until sunset on Saturday.

The Burial

Anciently, people used spices and ointments to prepare for burial the bodies of those who had died. Only wealthy people were buried in tombs. Jesus' tomb had never been used. The round stone that covered the doorway would most likely have been held in place by a track, also made of stone (Holzapfel et al., *World*, 144).

After Jesus died on the cross, a wealthy man named Joseph of Arimathea went to Pilate and begged to take the body of Jesus. Joseph was a leader among the Jews, but he did not agree with what they had done, and he wanted to give Jesus a proper burial. Along with his friend Nicodemus, Joseph took Jesus' body to a cave, carved out of a rock, that would have been Joseph's own tomb. Nicodemus brought a mixture of spices to prepare Jesus' body before he and Joseph wrapped it in linen burial clothes. A short distance away, Mary Magdalene and other faithful women watched as Joseph and Nicodemus hurried to bury Jesus' body before the Sabbath began.

The next morning, the Sabbath day, the chief priests and Pharisees went to Pilate. Calling Jesus a deceiver, or a liar, they told Pilate that Jesus had prophesied that he would rise from the tomb in three days. They worried that his disciples would steal his body and say that he had risen from the dead. They asked that the tomb be securely guarded. Pilate told them to do what they felt was necessary. Guards were placed at the tomb, and the stone across the door was sealed shut.

Early on the morning after the Sabbath, Mary Magdalene and other faithful women brought additional sweet spices to care for Jesus' body. As they walked toward the tomb, they wondered how they would move the large stone from the door. But when they arrived, they found that the stone had already been rolled away—and two angels in long white robes were sitting on it. The women were startled, but the angels told them not to fear and that Jesus was not dead. They showed the women the place where the Lord's body had lain, which was now empty, and told them to go and tell the apostles that Jesus had risen.

Both joyful and fearful because of all that they had seen and heard, Mary Magdalene and the other women ran to tell the apostles. Peter and John ran back to the tomb with them. Just as the women had described, the stone was rolled away and the tomb was empty, except for the linens that had covered Jesus' body.

Peter and John returned to their homes, but Mary Magdalene stayed by the tomb. Weeping, she looked into the tomb again, and she saw two angels dressed in white. One sat at the head, and the other sat at the feet of the place where Jesus had lain. They asked Mary why she was weeping. She replied that she was afraid someone had taken Jesus' body away, and she did not know where to find it.

When she turned away from the tomb, Mary saw a Man standing nearby. She did not recognize Him at first, and she thought He was the gardener. He asked her why she was crying, and she asked Him to tell her where she could find Jesus' body. Then the Man simply said, "Mary," and she turned to look at Him. She exclaimed, "Rabboni!" which means "Master." It was Jesus, and He had risen from the grave. As He had promised, on the third day after He died, He was alive again!

The Resurrected Jesus Visits His Disciples

Emmaus

The exact site of the village of Emmaus is unknown, but Luke tells us that Emmaus was "threescore furlongs," or about seven and a half miles from Jerusalem (Luke 24:13). By the time the disciples walked to Emmaus and back to Jerusalem that night, they had traveled a distance of about fifteen miles.

Honeycomb

Bees form hexagonal, or six-sided, cells in which to store the honey they produce. A cluster of these cells is called a honeycomb. Considered a delicacy by those in ancient times, honeycomb is served even today as a delicious appetizer or dessert.

The morning the resurrected Jesus appeared to Mary Magdalene became known as the first Sunday. During the afternoon of that same day, two of Jesus' disciples were on their way to a village called Emmaus. As they walked, they talked and tried to understand the events of recent days: how Jesus had been crucified and buried, and how on the third day some of his disciples had said they had seen the risen Lord. Suddenly, Jesus came near and began walking with them. He asked them why they seemed so sad. They did not recognize Him. They thought He was a stranger, and they began to tell Him all the things that had happened and how confused they felt.

Jesus listened to them for a time, and then He told them that it was necessary for all of these things to happen so that Christ could receive His crown of glory with His Father in Heaven. Beginning with Moses and continuing through all that the prophets had taught, Jesus showed the disciples how the scriptures testify of Christ. As the disciples listened, their hearts burned within them, and they knew that what this Man was teaching was true. But they still did not know who He was.

When they arrived in Emmaus, the disciples urged the stranger to stay with them for the evening meal. As they sat down to eat, Jesus blessed and broke the bread into pieces and served it to them. Suddenly, they realized who He was—and why they felt a burning in their hearts when He talked with them! Then Jesus immediately disappeared from their sight.

Without delay, the two disciples returned to Jerusalem to tell the apostles what had happened. They found the apostles inside a closed room, still afraid of what the angry Jewish leaders might do. As the two disciples reported the things they had seen and heard, Jesus appeared in the room. Everyone was afraid at first, but He said to them, "Peace be unto you."

He invited them to see and touch the prints of the nails in His hands and feet, explaining to them that a spirit does not have flesh and bones as they could see He had. He asked them if they had any food for Him to eat. They brought Him a piece of fish and a honeycomb, and He ate it, showing them He was their living Lord. Jesus helped them understand the scriptures and how the prophecies concerning His life, death, and resurrection had been fulfilled. He gave them instructions, and He blessed them. And then He departed.

The Ascension

During the forty days after He rose from the dead, Jesus made appearances to His apostles and other devoted disciples. On one occasion, Peter and some of the apostles had been fishing on the Sea of Galilee all night long. As morning came, they still had not caught anything. Jesus stood on the shore and called to them, but they did not recognize Him. He told them to cast their nets on the other side of the boat. When they did, their nets were immediately filled with fish. Only then did they realize it was Jesus who had called to them. Peter couldn't wait for the boat to reach the shore. He threw off his coat, dived in the water, and swam toward the Savior. The others came in the boat, dragging 153 fish in their net.

When they landed, the apostles saw that Jesus had lit a fire and cooked fish and bread for them. After they had finished eating, Jesus turned to Peter and asked him, "Lovest thou me?" Peter answered, "Yea, Lord, thou knowest that I love thee." Jesus said, "Feed my lambs." Then Jesus asked him the same question again, and Peter gave the same answer. This time, Jesus said, "Feed my sheep." Finally, a third time Jesus asked Peter if he loved Him. Peter, now somewhat uneasy, answered, "Lord, thou knowest all things. Thou knowest that I love thee." And Jesus repeated, "Feed my sheep." He wanted Peter—and all of the apostles—to understand that their mission was to serve and teach God's children everywhere. Jesus said to them, "Go ye into all the world, and preach the gospel to every creature."

During those forty days, Jesus had walked with the apostles, talked with them, and blessed them. Finally the day came when He told them He would soon be leaving them. He promised them that when He was gone, they would receive the Holy Ghost to help and comfort them. After He had spoken these words, the apostles watched as a cloud appeared and received Jesus into heaven. Two angels dressed in white also appeared and asked the apostles why they were looking up to heaven. The angels assured them that, in the same way that Jesus had left, He would someday reappear and return to earth again.

The Lord's Visitations

There are eleven recorded instances of Jesus appearing to the people during the forty days between His resurrection and His ascension into heaven. Sometimes He appeared to groups, even to as many as five hundred people at once (1 Corinthians 15:6), and other times He appeared to individuals, such as when He visited Peter (Luke 24:34) (Talmage, *Jesus the Christ,* 699).

The Apostle Thomas

The first time the resurrected Lord appeared to His apostles in the room with closed doors, Thomas was not present. Eight days later, when Jesus appeared to them again, Thomas was there. Jesus invited Thomas to touch His hands and His side to know that He had been resurrected. After doing this, Thomas knew that he had seen the risen Lord. Jesus taught that "blessed are they that have not seen, and yet have believed" (John 20:24–29).

The Apostles Lead the Church

Day of Pentecost

Fifty days, or seven weeks, after the Passover feast, Jews observed a holiday known as Pentecost, sometimes called the Feast of Harvest or the Feast of Weeks. During this time, grain was harvested, and offerings and sacrifices were made to God to thank Him for His blessings (Bible Dictionary, 673; *Life and Teachings* manual, 243–44).

Even though the apostles were sad that Jesus was no longer with them, they felt joy in knowing that He lived again. Because He had conquered death, all people would eventually be resurrected. After death, spirits and bodies would someday be reunited, never to be separated again.

The apostles returned to Jerusalem and gathered once again in the upper room. One hundred twenty of the faithful followers of Jesus Christ met with them and joined with them in prayer. Peter led a discussion about replacing the apostle Judas Iscariot, who was now dead. After asking the Lord to direct them, Peter and the other apostles felt that a disciple named Matthias was the one who should be chosen. Matthias became one of the twelve with a special calling to testify of Jesus Christ to all people.

About nine days after Jesus ascended into heaven, the apostles gathered again to celebrate Pentecost, or the Feast of Harvest. As they came together in a spirit of love and unity, the apostles were filled with the Holy Ghost. As Jesus had promised, they were blessed with power from God. The sound of a rushing, mighty wind came from heaven and filled the house where they were sitting, and they saw heaven-sent flames of fire that

rested on each of them but did not burn. The apostles were so filled with the Holy Ghost that they began to speak in other languages.

Word spread throughout the city, and people gathered outside the house where the apostles were staying. People from many different nations, speaking many different languages, lived in the city, and when the apostles spoke to them, everyone understood their words, no matter what language they spoke.

The people were amazed and felt the power of the Holy Ghost. Peter stood to teach them. He spoke of Jesus Christ and His death and resurrection and quoted many things the prophets had foretold. The people's hearts were touched, and they asked the apostles what they needed to do. "Repent," Peter replied, "and be baptized every one of you in the name of Jesus Christ for the remission of sins, and ye shall receive the gift of the Holy Ghost." Many of the people gladly received Peter's words, and on that day about three thousand were baptized.

First Presidency of the Church

Peter became the head of the Church after Jesus ascended to heaven. Today, we would call him the President of the Church, and James and John would be the equivalent of his counselors in the First Presidency (Ogden and Skinner, *Acts,* 27).

Peter Performs Miracles

Simon and the Priesthood

An unrighteous man named Simon lived in Samaria. He wanted the power that Peter and the apostles had, and he offered them money if they would give him the priesthood. They explained that the priesthood cannot be bought or sold. Only through proper authority and righteous living can a man have priesthood power (Acts 8:18–24).

Peter and the apostles traveled to many places, preaching the gospel of Jesus Christ and performing miracles in His name. One day, as they were on their way to the temple, Peter and John met a man who had never been able to walk. Every day, the man was carried to the gate of the temple, where he sat and asked people for money. Peter and John stopped to talk with the man. When he asked them for money, Peter told the man to look up at them. Peter explained that he did not have any silver or gold, but he would give the man what he had to offer.

Peter said to the man, "In the name of Jesus Christ of Nazareth, rise up and walk." Peter took the man by the right hand and lifted him up. Immediately, the man received strength in his feet and ankles. He leaped up, stood on his feet, and walked into the temple with Peter and John, praising God and rejoicing. The people recognized him as the man who daily sat by the gate of the temple. They gathered around him and marveled at his miraculous healing.

Peter went on a missionary journey to the city of Lydda. There he met a man named Aeneas, who had lain in bed, sick with palsy, for eight years. Peter said to Aeneas, "Jesus Christ maketh thee whole: arise, and make thy bed." Aeneas immediately arose and was healed.

In Joppa, not far from Lydda, lived a faithful woman named Tabitha, also known as Dorcas, who went about serving others. She helped the poor and made clothing for widows. When she became ill and died, two men were sent to Peter to ask if he would come quickly to Joppa. When Peter arrived, the widows and others Tabitha had served were weeping and mourning over her. Peter asked them all to leave the room, and he knelt down by Tabitha's bed to pray. Then, turning to her body on the bed, Peter commanded her to arise. Tabitha opened her eyes, and when she saw Peter, she sat up. He gave her his hand and helped her to stand. Peter called her friends back into the room and presented her to them. Tabitha was alive!

Joppa and Lydda

An important seaport in ancient times, Joppa was located about thirty miles northwest of Jerusalem along the shores of the Mediterranean Sea. Lydda, nearer to Jerusalem and the capital of a small state, was about ten miles southeast of Joppa (Madsen, "Women," 40).

Peter and Cornelius

Simon the Tanner

In Joppa, Peter was a guest in the seaside home of a good man named Simon, who was a tanner. A tanner works with animal hides to turn them into leather.

Cornelius was a good man. He was also a Roman centurion, or a soldier in command of one hundred men. Cornelius was not a Jew, but he believed in God and was always prayerful. He gave generously to the poor and tried to live righteously. One day, while Cornelius was fasting and praying, an angel of God came to him in a vision and told him that God was pleased with him. The angel told Cornelius to send his servants to the city of Joppa and ask for a man named Simon Peter. The angel explained that Peter would tell Cornelius what he should do. Cornelius was obedient. Immediately, he sent two servants and one of his soldiers to find Peter.

On the same day that Cornelius's servants were traveling toward Joppa, Peter went to pray on the housetop of the home where he had been staying. After a while, he grew very hungry. As he was waiting for food to be prepared, Peter had a vision. He saw the heavens open, and a giant sheet came down to earth holding all kinds of animals and birds. A voice instructed Peter to rise, kill one of the animals, and eat it. Peter did not want to eat any of the animals he saw in the vision. According to Jewish law, the animals in the sheet were considered unclean, and only Gentiles, or people who had not made a covenant with God, ate those animals. But the voice explained to Peter that if God declares that something is clean, it is clean and is no longer forbidden. The vision was repeated three times, and then the sheet was taken up into heaven.

While Peter was pondering the meaning of the vision, the servants of Cornelius arrived at the gate. The Spirit of the Lord spoke to Peter and told him that three men were waiting to see him. He was told not to doubt but to go with the men because the Lord had sent them.

Peter went down to meet the messengers. He asked them their purpose in coming. They explained that an angel told their master, Cornelius, a good and honest Roman, to send for Peter to teach him. At last, Peter understood the meaning of his vision: the gospel was to be taught to the Gentiles as well as the Jews. The gospel of Jesus Christ was for all people.

The next morning, Peter went with the soldier and the servants to Joppa to meet Cornelius. When Peter entered the house, Cornelius fell at his feet and worshipped him. Peter helped Cornelius stand up and told him he did not need to worship Peter because Peter was a man like himself. Peter taught the gospel of Jesus Christ to the friends and family of Cornelius who had gathered in his home. Peter said that now he understood that God does not value any of His children more than the others. While he was speaking, the Holy Ghost came upon his Gentile listeners, and Peter commanded that Cornelius and all those who believed should be baptized.

Gentiles

In the scriptures, the term *Gentiles* sometimes refers to people who were not Jews, and sometimes it refers to people who were not Israelites. It also may simply refer to people who do not have the gospel (Bible Dictionary, 679).

Peter and the Apostles in Prison

Sadducees

The Sadducees were a small group of wealthy and powerful Jewish leaders who were in charge of maintaining the temple. They upheld the old, written law and did not adopt the oral laws as the Pharisees did. They did not believe in resurrection, angels, or an afterlife (Bible Dictionary, 767).

The Apostle James

James, the brother of John, was one of the original twelve apostles. King Herod ordered that he be killed by the sword (Acts 12:1–2).

Peter and the other apostles taught many people about Jesus Christ and His resurrection. They performed miracles, as Jesus did, and the people listened when they taught and testified of Jesus Christ. Thousands of Jews became Christians. The priests, Pharisees, and Sadducees were afraid they would lose their power over the people. They put Peter and John in prison. That night, an angel of the Lord opened the doors and led them out of the prison. The angel told them to go and preach in the temple.

The Jewish leaders were surprised to see Peter and John teaching in the temple courtyard again. They took them before the Jewish council and commanded them to stop teaching about Jesus Christ. But Peter and the others answered that they must obey God rather than men. The priests commanded the apostles to be beaten. Then they once more ordered them not to preach in the name of Jesus, and they let them go. Peter and the others left the council rejoicing that they had been called upon to make sacrifices in the name of Christ—and they continued to preach about Him in the temple and in people's homes.

Sometime later, during Passover season, King Herod again put Peter in prison. The faithful members of the Church prayed for Peter without ceasing. The night before Herod was going to present Peter to the Jews for punishment, he commanded Peter to be bound with chains and forced to sleep between two soldiers, with more soldiers guarding the prison door. During the night, an angel of the Lord came to Peter. A light shone in the dark prison, and the angel woke Peter, telling him to rise quickly. When Peter stood, the chains miraculously fell from his hands. The angel told Peter to put on his robe and his sandals and follow him out of the prison. Peter followed the angel, wondering if he were dreaming. Together they walked past the soldiers and into the street. Then the angel departed, and Peter knew that he had not been dreaming and that the Lord had delivered him out of the hands of the king and the Jews.

Peter quickly went to the home of Mary, the mother of a disciple named Mark, where the people had gathered to pray. He knocked on the door of the gate, and a young woman named Rhoda went to open it. She was so glad to hear Peter's voice that she ran back inside to tell the others—leaving Peter at the gate. The people thought Rhoda was crazy because they were sure Peter was still in prison. But Rhoda insisted that it was Peter at the gate. Peter kept knocking, and when they finally opened the door, the people were astonished to see him. Peter told them everything that had happened and how the Lord had delivered him from prison once again.

The next morning, when Herod discovered that Peter had escaped, he examined the prison guards and then commanded that they be put to death. In time, however, God struck Herod with a horrible disease, and he died, and Peter and the other apostles continued to testify of Jesus Christ and preach His gospel.

The Stoning of Stephen

Ananias and Sapphira

When the apostles led the Church, members covenanted to share what they had with each other. A man named Ananias and his wife, Sapphira, sold some of their land, but they kept part of the money for themselves instead of giving it to the Church. Peter discerned their dishonesty. When he asked Ananias and Sapphira why they had lied to God, both of them fell down and died (Acts 4:32–5:11).

As the apostles traveled from city to city teaching the gospel, many more people became followers of Jesus Christ. Because there were so many to teach and to help, some of the disciples became concerned that the widows might be forgotten. The twelve apostles called the people together and chose seven honest and wise men to care for the needy. Hands were laid on their heads, and they were called to serve the people.

Stephen was one of the seven who were called. He was an especially good man, filled with faith and with the Spirit of the Lord. He performed miracles and great works among the people. Some of the leaders of the

synagogue became jealous of Stephen's wisdom and power. They stirred up the people and the elders and brought him before the Jewish council. False witnesses told lies about Stephen, saying that he had said and done things that were against the law. While they threw their angry accusations at him, Stephen remained calm and was filled with the Spirit. His face became radiant like the face of an angel.

When the high priest asked Stephen to answer the charges against him, Stephen began to speak. He reviewed the history of the Israelites and God's dealings with them. He boldly reminded them that their people had turned away from God and had refused to listen to the Holy Ghost and that they had persecuted the prophets and even betrayed and murdered Jesus Christ. Stephen's words cut the Jews to their hearts. They did not want to hear him speak the truth. They were so angry they were like wild beasts.

But Stephen was filled with the Holy Ghost. As the Jews shouted at him, Stephen steadily looked up to heaven. He saw the heavens open, and he saw the resurrected Jesus standing on the right side of Heavenly Father. When Stephen told the priests and elders what he saw, they cried out with a loud voice, covered their ears, and rushed at him. They forced him out of the city and threw stones at him, wanting to kill him. At last, the wounded Stephen cried out to God, saying, "Lord Jesus, receive my spirit." He knelt down and, with a loud voice, asked the Lord to forgive his attackers. And when he had done this, Stephen died.

The Temple in Jerusalem

The temple in Jerusalem was a center for missionary activity as well as for worship, and it remained an important gathering place for the early saints. The apostles preached on the steps of the temple, and it was a place of revelation where the Spirit of the Lord could be felt. Later, however, the people disobeyed the commandments, and God's presence left His house. Eventually, the Romans attacked Jerusalem and destroyed the temple (Holzapfel et al., *World,* 160–61).

The Apostle Paul

Preaching in the Synagogue

In nearly every town where Jews lived, there was a Jewish meetinghouse called a synagogue. Early Christian missionaries, such as Peter and Paul, preached the gospel in synagogues because these were places where people gathered (Bible Dictionary, 778).

Saul Becomes Paul

In his early life, this apostle was known by his Hebrew name, Saul. When he became a missionary for Jesus Christ, he was known as Paul, the Latin version of his name (Acts 13:9; Bible Dictionary, 742).

As the disciple Stephen was being stoned to death, a young man named Saul stood by and watched. Saul was a leader among the Jews, a Pharisee, who threatened to put the followers of Jesus Christ in prison or, worse, to death. One day, while he was on his way to Damascus to arrest Christians there, Saul suddenly saw a light from heaven. He fell to the earth and heard a voice that asked him, "Saul, why persecutest thou me?" Saul asked who was speaking, and the voice answered, "I am Jesus whom thou persecutest."

The men who journeyed with Saul stood speechless. They saw the light but they did not hear the voice that spoke to him. Trembling and astonished, Saul asked Jesus what He would have him do. The Lord told him to continue to the city of Damascus, where he would receive instructions. Saul stood and opened his eyes, but he could no longer see. His friends led him by the hand into the city. Saul was blind for three days, eating and drinking nothing in all that time.

In Damascus, a disciple of Jesus Christ named Ananias had a vision in which the Lord spoke to him. The Lord told Ananias to go to a certain house on a certain street. There he would find a man named Saul, who had seen a vision in which a man named Ananias came to restore his sight! When Ananias heard the name "Saul," he protested at first because he knew this man had tried to destroy the followers of Christ. But the Lord told Ananias not to fear and that Saul was a chosen vessel, called by the Lord to testify of Him to the world.

Ananias obeyed the Lord. He found Saul and laid his hands on Saul's head. He told Saul that the Lord had sent him to restore Saul's vision and bless him with the Holy Ghost. Immediately, Saul could see again. He arose and asked to be baptized. More than anything else, he now wanted to be a true follower of Jesus Christ.

Saul stayed with the disciples in Damascus for a period of time, and he preached in the synagogues, testifying that Jesus Christ is the Son of God. At first, the people were amazed that Saul, the Jew who tried to arrest people for believing in Jesus, was now His disciple. His testimony that Jesus is the Christ grew so powerful, and so many people began listening to him that the Jewish leaders became angry. They plotted to kill him and watched for him by the city gates night and day. The disciples took Saul in the night, put him in a basket, and lowered him over the city wall. He escaped safely to Jerusalem.

Saul, the converted Pharisee, became known as Paul, the great missionary and apostle of the Lord Jesus Christ. He performed miracles in Jesus' name, and many people were converted by his preaching. Paul had adventures on land and sea as he traveled to many lands testifying of Jesus Christ. Even when he was cast into prison, he spent his time writing letters to teach and strengthen the saints. Paul remained faithful to the Lord until the end of his days.

Acknowledgments

After spending the past two years immersed in the stories and teachings of the Old and New Testaments, I have adopted a favorite set of metaphors: "Manna" in the Old Testament and "The Bread of Life" in the New Testament. I have a strong testimony of daily sustenance. The scriptures feed our souls, and we need that "food" every day. If we turn to Him, the Lord really does sustain us in all our efforts, not the least of which is writing a book. My first and most heartfelt acknowledgment is to the Lord for His daily sustenance.

I feel to acknowledge the scholars of ancient scripture who helped bring historical accuracy and interest to this book. While their contributions are annotated throughout, I want to thank them for doing the hard work of scholarly research and writing. Their contributions are invaluable.

I gratefully acknowledge the devoted people in Deseret Book's publishing department. First, I want to thank Jana Erickson, who guided this book through to completion. I especially want to thank my talented and skilled editor, Vicki Parry, whose watchcare made lasting impressions upon the pages of this book. I also want to thank Rachael Ward for her professional typesetting. And I am so thankful to graphic designer Shauna Gibby, who directed the visual elements of this book.

I am even more awe-inspired than before by Brian Call's illustrations—he truly brought the stories to life.

Finally, I want to thank my husband for his love and support. No one knows better than he does how much time and effort went into this book. I also want to thank my children. Even though only two children remain at home, all of them cheered for my best efforts from near and far. Such a spiritually sensitive project simply could not have been undertaken without the steady flow of love and support I received from my family.

—Karmel Newell

I am grateful to a loving Heavenly Father who has helped me accomplish this wonderful project. Special thanks to my wife, Michelle, and my family for sacrificing their time with me while I painted. Also, many thanks to my family, ward members, and students for being such great models and for helping me bring the Bible stories to life.

—Brian Call

Sources

"About Patriarchal Blessings." *New Era,* March 2004, 32–35.

Bible Dictionary. King James Bible, LDS edition. Salt Lake City: The Church of Jesus Christ of Latter-day Saints, 1979.

Brown, S. Kent, Richard Neitzel Holzapfel, and Dawn C. Pheysey. *Beholding Salvation: The Life of Christ in Word and Image.* Salt Lake City: Deseret Book, 2006.

Hastings, Selina. *The Children's Illustrated Bible.* New York: Dorling Kindersley, 2004.

Holzapfel, Richard Neitzel, Dana M. Pike, and David Rolph Seely. *Jehovah and the World of the Old Testament.* Salt Lake City: Deseret Book, 2009.

Hymns of The Church of Jesus Christ of Latter-day Saints. Salt Lake City: The Church of Jesus Christ of Latter-day Saints, 1985.

lds.org, *Guide to the Scriptures.*

The Life and Teachings of Jesus and His Apostles [student manual]. Salt Lake City: The Church of Jesus Christ of Latter-day Saints, 1979.

Madsen, Ann. "Cameos: The Women of the New Testament," *Ensign,* September 1975, 40–43.

McConkie, Bruce R. "Christ and the Creation." *Ensign*, June 1982, 9–15.

McConkie, Bruce R. *Doctrinal New Testament Commentary,* 3 vols. Salt Lake City: Bookcraft, 1965.

Ogden, D. Kelly. *Where Jesus Walked: The Land and Culture of New Testament Times.* Salt Lake City: Deseret Book, 1991.

Ogden, D. Kelly, and Andrew C. Skinner. *Verse by Verse: Acts through Revelation.* Salt Lake City: Deseret Book, 1998.

Ogden, D. Kelly, and Andrew C. Skinner. *Verse by Verse: The Four Gospels.* Salt Lake City: Deseret Book, 2006.

Old Testament Student Manual: Genesis–2 Samuel (Religion 301). Salt Lake City: The Church of Jesus Christ of Latter-day Saints, 1980.

Old Testament Student Manual: 1 Kings–Malachi (Religion 302). Salt Lake City: The Church of Jesus Christ of Latter-day Saints, 1981.

Olson, Camille Fronk. *Women of the Old Testament.* Salt Lake City: Deseret Book, 2009.

Parry, Jay A., and Donald W. Parry. *Understanding the Parables of Jesus Christ.* Salt Lake City: Deseret Book, 2006.

Proctor, Maurine Jensen, and Scot Facer Proctor. *Source of the Light: A Witness and Testimony of Jesus Christ, the Savior and Redeemer of All.* Salt Lake City: Deseret Book, 1992.

Rasmussen, Ellis T. *A Latter-day Saint Commentary on the Old Testament.* Salt Lake City: Deseret Book, 2001.

Smith, Joseph. *Teachings of the Prophet Joseph Smith.* Selected by Joseph Fielding Smith. Salt Lake City: Deseret Book, 1976.

Talmage, James E. *The House of the Lord: A Study of Holy Sanctuaries, Ancient and Modern.* Salt Lake City: Deseret Book, 1976.

Talmage, James E. *Jesus the Christ.* Salt Lake City: The Deseret News, 1916.

Valetta, Thomas R. et al., eds. *The Old Testament for Latter-day Saint Families: Illustrated King James Version with Helps for Children.* Salt Lake City: Deseret Book, 2005.

Additional Illustration Credits

Alexander Bida/Wikimedia/public domain, 135

Chabad.org/public domain, 108

Caravaggio/Wikimedia/public domain, 114, 151

Gustave Doré/public domain, 40 bottom, 160

Shauna Gibby, 66, 73 bottom

Hanay/Wikimedia/rights released, 61

Jozef Israëls/Wikimedia/public domain, 20

Jan Luyken/Wikimedia/public domain, 128

Material Culture Auction Dept., Philadelphia, PA., 62

Mewasul/Wikimedia/rights released, 139 top

Scott Proctor (*Source of the Light*), 91

Reliquary of Brescia/Wikimedia/public domain, 158

Rembrandt/Wikimedia/public domain, 149 top

Julius Schnorr von Carolsfeld/Wikimedia/public domain, 7

Shutterstock.com, 4 (Clint Cearley), 14 (Marina Mariya), 37 (Salajean), 40 top (Roman Sigaev), 43 (Morphart Creation), 45 (Bayanova Svetlana), 46 (Rachelle Burnside), 48 (Eric Isselee), 51 (hjschneider), 52 (Lowe R. Llaguno), 53 (arindambanerjee), 54 top (Baloncici), 73 top (Algars Reinholds), 77 bottom (James Steidl), 90 bottom (Ahmad A Atwah), 92 (Aprilphoto), 95 top (Aprilphoto), 97 (Christian Vinces), 107 top (Sergio Stakhnyk), 113 (Glenn R. Specht), 118 (Palsarn Praha), 119 (Kachalkina Veronika), 122 (alersandr hunta), 123 (Ryan Rodrick Beller), 124 (Kobby Dagan), 127 (Lee Prince), 129 (Yingko), 137 (Tom Bird), 146 top (Africa Studio), 146 bottom (Yosefer), 150 (Lorraine Kourafas), 156 bottom (Zvonimir Atletic)

Thinkquest.org/public domain, 109

Thinkstock, 3, 6, 9, 11, 12, 15, 16, 17, 18, 19, 21, 22, 24, 25, 26, 28, 30, 33, 34, 35, 38, 49, 54 bottom, 57, 58, 59, 64, 65, 67, 68, 70, 72, 74, 75, 76, 77 top, 79, 80, 83, 85, 86, 87 top, 87 bottom, 88, 89, 90 top, 95 bottom, 96, 99, 100, 101, 102, 105, 107 bottom, 110, 112, 115, 117, 120, 125, 131, 132 (top), 132 (bottom), 134, 136, 139 bottom, 140, 144 top, 144 bottom, 149 bottom, 153, 154, 159

Tissot/Wikimedia/public domain, 156 top

Unknown artist/Wikimedia/public domain, 142

Index